The
Rapture of the Deep

AND OTHER

DIVE STORIES

You Probably Shouldn't Know

By

MICHAEL ZINSLEY

ABOUT THE BOOK

Journey with scuba instructor Michael Zinsley as he dives his way through 16 countries, rubbing shoulders with the locals and mixing underwater adventure with after-hours escapades.

The Rapture of the Deep is fast paced and rich in content, consisting of: humorous anecdotes, insightful histories, underwater descriptions, and terrifying close calls. The diving stories relate events seen once in a thousand dives. Native cultures are revealed with an awareness that only someone who has lived in those lands can describe. The book's lighter side is the combination of underwater adventure mixed with after-hours escapades (imagine Cousteau extending his documentaries to include closing time in the local bars). The descriptions of coral reef life are written in a way that non-diving readers will be as intrigued as the experts.

Featuring stories from:

Antigua, Australia, Bermuda, Bonaire, California, Fiji, Guam, Indonesia, Malaysia, New Zealand, Palau, Philippines, Ponape, Saint Lucia, Thailand, Tonga, Truk, the U.S. Virgin Islands, Vanuatu, Western Samoa, and Yap.

" . . . we are a new race of seamen. We must learn to take care of ourselves among the waves and winds on the surface, as mariners have always done, but also in the darkness and among the dangers beneath the surface of the water. To us, the complete seaman is the one who is perfectly at home both on and under the surface." Jacques

"A trip is a blank canvas that can be painted any way you like." Megs

"You'll do what you want to do." Jim's axiom

"Life is uncertain. Eat your dessert first." Bill

Sunset over Truk Lagoon

TABLE OF CONTENTS

ACKNOWLEDGMENTS

For computer help, tireless editing, and encouragement when I needed it most, stellar thanks to:

Erika Bauer
Jill Boroski
David Caccamo
Steve Cooke
Dwight Lewis
Bill Mallchok
Bill McMahon
Maria Porges
Rachel Shahinian
Stephanie Susnjara
Jill Toyoshiba
Richard and Lynne Zinsley

Also Thanks To:

Peet's Coffee
Bintang Brewery
Khun Sang Thip for bursts of inspiration
. . . and all those who provided me with material by taking a dive course even though they couldn't tie their shoes.

Truk shipwreck photo credit to Manfred Rhode.
All other photos are from author's collection.

"I've seen things here that I could never possibly have imagined, and I'm a guy with a pretty broad imagination." Gene

As I turned my student's air off, I watched her eyes, waiting for a reaction. The needle on the gauge in front of her plunged to zero as she sucked hard on her mouthpiece. When she realized that there was nothing left to breathe, she looked at me quizzically, then shot to the surface. Fortunately, we were in a shallow training pool, and not the ocean.

"Why'd you come up?" I asked.

"I ran out of air."

"You didn't run out of air. I turned it off."

"What the hell did you do that for?"

"It's the skill we're practicing. You're supposed to signal 'out of air' and let me turn it back on. Let's try it again."

It had been a long season, and it was frustrating to spend extra time with an inattentive student. (Used together, the words "air," "off," "under," and "water" usually penetrate even the deepest of daydreams.) As she put her mask and regulator back in the appropriate places for her brief descent, I took a deep breath and reminded myself that overall, I still loved what I was doing. Glancing at the high limestone cliffs and jungle surrounding the tropical resort, I reflected for a moment on the events of the previous eight years and what had led me to that pool, ten thousand miles from home.

It was an inspiration that started while I was working as a high school teacher in Los Angeles. I enjoyed teaching, but stressful conditions made me miserable. Feeling trapped by the city, I spent evenings watching sunsets from my balcony while televisions flickered on the window shades of the apartments around me. I saw my lifetime as a book, but my future was written before me as a tale as monotonous as those of my neighbors. I dreamed of an edition filled with a series of adventures, tightly packed to fit into my given volume of life. Those porch sunsets beckoned me across the ocean, to mysterious lands where bills, taxes, and dull routine would disappear.

At the end of the school year, I accepted a position as a professional mountain guide, but I soon realized it wasn't what I sought. Hacking and thrashing my way up some godforsaken mound of ice-covered rock with clumsy customers on the end of my rope had lost its appeal. Continuous weeks above timberline left little time for a social life. I would march to each summit secretly hoping that the dream girl I had never met might somehow find out about my heroic ascent and surrender herself to me in fairy-tale awe. Instead, I returned from every plod to share a cold wet tent with another male climber who also hadn't bathed in awhile. To top things off, the pay was so lousy, we had to live out of our cars on days off.

It was time to continue my quest for Eden, and becoming a diving instructor on a tropical island seemed to be an ideal choice. I could still have adventure, pursue my dream girl fantasy by investigating the diver-as-playboy stereotype, and be in a place where a hammock and a piña colada awaited me at the end of each day instead of a damp tent. Also, unlike mountain guiding, if inexperienced customers inadvertently tried to kill themselves with uncoordinated antics, I wouldn't be tied to them.

However, I quickly discovered Scrooge-like dive shop owners bent on working me to exhaustion during the crush of high season, a few impossible to please customers, and a tedious month-after-month cycle of twenty dives per week. Nobody mentioned long evenings filling tanks, unclogging boat toilets, or sweeping floors when I was signing on the dotted line. I started to miss family, friends, hot showers, and Mexican food. It also seemed wasteful that after going to engineering school, the only ratio I was calculating was rum to pineapple juice.

In New York City, I once complained to a friend over dinner about slaving for an incompetent shop owner in the Caribbean. He leaned over the table and pointed his finger at my face. "Hey! They could whip you down there, and it would still be better than wearing a suit to work in Manhattan every day!"

He was right. I wouldn't have traded lives with him under any circumstance. I was far from the daily grind of freeway rush hour, in a place where vacationers from all over the world made an effort to maximize their fun. Winter had friends at home bundled in coats while I flourished in the warm caresses of the trade winds. Brilliant starry nights spent outside under the Southern Cross also reminded me that I was doing fine right where I was.

I also enjoyed introducing people to the underwater world and watching their excitement grow as they discovered it. Over four-day courses, I helped them hone their skills until they could safely dive without me. My approach was left over from the mountain days — leading innocents into a formidable challenge and working them through it to build the confidence they needed. Weakness was their greatest enemy. Self-sufficient adventure was their greatest thrill. No whining was allowed.

Students form the backbone of the sport diving industry. Although most never do more than twenty dives in their lives, their sheer numbers support the trade with further tuition, equipment sales, and boat trips. The professionals reap the proceeds: divemasters, the ski bums of the tropics, function as trip leaders and underwater tour guides. Instructors, licensed to teach through certifying organizations, make more money, but find themselves diving in swimming pools half the time. Shop owners are instructors turned businessmen. They optimize their time by concentrating on greenbacks rather than the emerald hues of parrotfish.

The following chapters are a blend of travel stories and anecdotes, most of which were written overseas. They start with my first dives ten years ago and proceed more or less chronologically as I metamorphosed from an impressionable neophyte into a veteran instructor. The change in my attitude during this time is reflected throughout the book. That is, the first stories generally explore the wonder and beauty of coral reefs, while hundreds of dives later, the tales focus less on the common sights and more on the customers, who provided an endless source of amusement. The locations change throughout the book as I explore dive sites in new countries: from Australia and the South Pacific, to the wonderland of Palau, over to the Caribbean, back to Palau, and finally to the unbelievably unfamiliar environment of Southeast Asia.

My visits to these lands varied from one week vacations to working stints of a year or more. Whether Palangi, Haole, Farang or Turis, the names all meant the same; I was the big white guest. I saw many vacationers projecting their own world onto the foreign environments they visited, thereby missing out on the full travel experience. Unlike them, I spent enough time in each country to become absorbed in the lives of the local people. In fact, I didn't have much choice. The surrounding cultures seized me and pinned me until I said "Uncle." This is the story of my encounters with these people, as well as the close calls, the humor, and the nomadic life of a professional diver.

PACIFIC ISLANDS

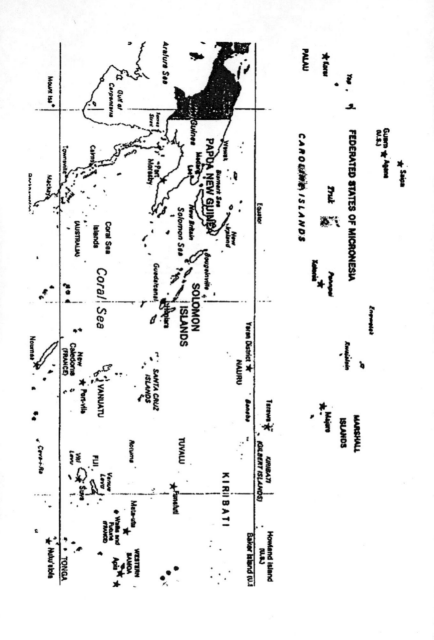

FEDERATED STATES OF MICRONESIA

IT'S YER SHOUT, MATE
Australia

"Germans are cranky because they're hungover all day. Aussies start drinking at breakfast and have a great time, all the time." Karry

"Q. In what month do Australians drink the least amount of beer?

A. February. It has the least amount of days." Mind Trap

May, 1988

"Where ya from, mate?"

"California."

"Oh, a Yank. Need a beer?"

"Sure."

My new friend gave the high sign to the bar and brought back four VBs (Victoria Bitters) for me and his two buddies. They opened the circle to let me join them and riddled me with questions as to why I was in their pub.

There were a few chest high tables in the room, but no stools. Music wasn't played, but the pub roared with happy-hour conversations. After taking a few sips from their stubbies (an Australian sip is approximately one-third of a beer) my companions ordered four more from the bar. I had certainly stumbled onto the right crowd on my first night in the outback, hospitable *and* generous. I did my best to keep up with their pace as a third round appeared. As soon as that one was finished, they watched me intently.

"What?"

"It's yer shout mate!"

Oh, so every one takes turns! I thought they were just being good hosts. It didn't take long to figure out that Aussies won't stand for beer moochers and will tell you when it is your turn to shout (buy) a round. This is dangerous in a large group because a half-dozen men will drink six, twelve, or eighteen beers as shouts go full circle. Very few stop after six.

Australia is a rough land. They have the worst droughts, hardest rains, and biggest mosquitoes – and the people aren't afraid to tell you so. They reflect their environment with parched humor and rough manners, but they also possess an uncommon friendliness.

I originally landed in Hobart, then hit Melbourne, Sydney, and Brisbane as I worked my way north towards the tropics. Travelers I met coming the other direction told me that *the* thing to do in Cairns was take a diving course. After surveying my funds, I decided to go for it. I was already an avid snorkeler, and scuba was the next logical step.

After a friendly chat with the Qantas crew on the flight from Brisbane to Cairns, I was handed eight unopened cans of Castlemaine XXXX (pronounced "Four X") as I left the plane. Sitting next to the driver on the bus into town, I offered him one of the beers.

He said, "Nah, I'm right, mate."

"Mind if I have one?"

"Won't bother me long as ya don't break out singing."

He let me off at the wharf where my first priority was finding a dive school. Across the street, the doors of *Dives Are Us* beckoned. The cheap prices indicated that the courses were over-packed with students, but I didn't care. I was on a budget. I just wanted to have fun and get a certification card. The price included six dives, a night dive, and an overnight boat trip to the Great Barrier Reef.

A sugar town turned to tourism, Cairns was a sad excuse for a tropical paradise – a mishmash of buildings pinned to the coastline by jungle covered hills. The Great Barrier Reef earned its name by keeping waves away from the shore, allowing mud flats to build up instead of sandy beaches. The neighborhood pubs were fun hangouts but the real action was clearly on the reef.

4

The next available dive course wasn't for two days, so I had time for some sightseeing away from the town. I hitched rides over the winding roads of rain-forested hills, through sugar cane plantations, and past stately homes built on raised posts to reduce summer heat and flood damage.

At the end of the day, I was hot and thirsty on the homestretch when an old ute (pickup truck) with three rough-looking characters in front stopped to give me a lift.

The driver said, "We're not going far, mate, just up to the pub."

"Perfect. I'll join you." I hopped in the back.

Terry, Johnny, and Ronny were cane cutters who had spent their lives working in the sugar fields. As soon as we got inside the pub, I knew what to do. I shouted the first round and was "in like Flynn" with them. ("Good on ya, Yank.") After a couple shouts, they invited me over to their place for tucker, and said I could throw out my swag in their caravan (have dinner and put my sleeping bag on the spare cot in their trailer for the night). We had a great meal of fried steak and onions . . . and beer, of course. Real bush-style living.

As I was leaving the next morning, Ronny asked me for advice. "The doc said fer me to lay off the piss cause me liver's crook, what d'yer reckon?" (The doctor said for me to quit drinking alcohol, because my liver is sick. What is your opinion?)

I poked under the right side of his rib cage with my finger, and he jumped back in pain.

"I think the doctor's right."

He didn't seem to think that was fair and protested, "I only drink ten beers a day!"

DIVE GODS
Cairns, Australia

"Australian foreplay? You know what that is. Nudge your bird and say, 'Are ya awake?'" Frank

Our huge dive class congregated at eight a.m. inside a concrete block room behind the dive shop. We crowded into high-school-style desk chairs while our instructor enlightened us with his wisdom. Frank was typical for a man of the region — cocky, macho, and always right. To us, he was Dive God.

Our first dive was blissful ignorant confusion at a small island not far from Cairns. Dive God filed us down a twenty-foot descent line onto an underwater mud flat. The only thing we did was practice skills and wait for the others, watching a single fish that wandered curiously around us. I wasn't disappointed, though; I was so high on the sensation of breathing under water that finding an empty soup can was exciting. The depths could now be pondered over time, instead of glimpsed on one breath.

The final dives were from a live-aboard boat on the Great Barrier Reef. The depths teemed with life and color — everything I had hoped for. Dive God led us through schools of batfish, along underwater canyons, and past walls that dropped vertically below us for a hundred feet. He showed us lobsters hiding under ledges, flowery tube worms that disappeared into their sheaths when touched, and fish carefully guarding their eggs. He pointed to a sea turtle as it paddled lazily past. Then he picked up the molted exoskeleton of a shrimp, a hollow twin that had been ditched by the growing animal. I felt welcome in that mysterious world, a place where creatures thought and behaved so differently, they might as well have been from another planet.

After one forty-minute tour, I still had air left, so I stayed nearby on a shallow reef as the others waited in line to climb the boat ladder. In front of me lay a Lilliputian coral garden. As I watched, my attention focused on minute details until I was seeing eye-to-eye with the community's members. Six inches in front of my mask, a shrimp the size of a pencil-tip busily groomed its head with its legs. Near it, a red blenny fish the size of a pen cap skittered back and forth on the square-inch doorstep of the hole it called home. It had a grasshopper-like head, bulging red-striped eyes, a full-lipped mouth, and two antennae — reminiscent of a 1950's sci-fi character. Its nervous twitching and frowning facial expression gave it a neurotic personality.

From a hole in the "roof" of the blenny's apartment block, a pair of fan-like "hands," each the size of a pinhead, reached out, grabbed a passing plankton, and pulled it down into a tiny shell that lined the hole. Looking inside, I discovered a crab-like face chomping away on the single-celled lunch. It was a barnacle, living in the permanent home it had bored in the coral. I felt like a kid on Christmas morning who had been good all year. When a surge of current reminded me that I was under water, I snapped out of my reverie and read that my air was low. I had to surface.

Because scuba diving came naturally to me, I got cocky and turned into a nightmarish student, jetting away from my buddy, chasing fish and turtles, and ducking into caves when Dive God wasn't looking. The maximum depth during the course was supposed to be sixty, but my excitement wouldn't let dive tables restrict me. I went to seventy-seven feet during a stingray chase through a wide rock fissure. (A week later, I looked down from the height of an eighth floor balcony, elated that the ominous distance below was equal to that depth.)

On my last dive, I saw my first shark, a whitetip hovering sixty feet in the distance. Fear and adrenaline coursed through my veins as I slowly moved out of its sight, grateful that it hadn't wandered closer upon seeing me.

After I was certified and let loose on the diving world, I went to the dive shop and started checking prices for another dive excursion around Cairns. A poster advertised DIVE THE COD HOLE. Underneath were photos of divers hand feeding

8

shrimp to Volkswagen-sized potato cod. Also pictured was the island, a jungled pinnacle of rock ringed by a reef and a powder-blue lagoon. A three-day two-night trip was three-hundred dollars on a live-aboard boat. I calculated that my time spent under water would cost fifty-dollars an hour on average. It didn't matter. I was hooked. Even though I was on a backpacker's budget, I didn't hesitate to pay it. Three years and several thousand dollars later, I became a divemaster to support my new addiction — similar to a junkie who starts dealing to get free drugs.

THE SUNKEN RAINBOW
New Zealand

"Forget about World Peace.
Visualize using your turn signal!" bumper sticker

"You can't sink a rainbow." That's a poetic slogan, but it looked pretty sunk when I saw it. On the night of July 10, 1985, an explosion blew a six-foot wide hole in the hull of the Rainbow Warrior while it was alongside an Auckland wharf. Within a minute, a second bomb administered the *coup de grace*. The Greenpeace ship quickly foundered in shallow water, drowning crew member Fernando Pereira.

The news traveled worldwide in hours. Morning editions around the globe featured photos of the 160-foot converted fishing trawler wallowed into the harbor mud with a slight list to starboard. Other than the high tide mark halfway up the superstructure, the activist's ship didn't appear to be damaged. The banner over the bridge proclaiming "Nuclear Free Pacific" broadcast its message more powerfully than ever.

It didn't take long to figure out that the blasts came from bombs placed on the keel, but who was responsible? The initial list of suspects was far from short. Greenpeace had been raising hell for six years against a dozen nations and many private interests, braving the business ends of whale harpoons, invading Russian fisheries, and protesting toxic waste dumping in the North Sea. The next Greenpeace mission was scheduled for Moruroa, command center for France's testing of nuclear weapons in the Tuamotu Archipelago of French Polynesia.

After two accidents in Moruroa in 1979 and 1981, plutonium had been detected in New Zealand fish. (Besides being radioactive, plutonium is extremely toxic. A thimble-full could potentially kill millions of people). The environmentally-

11

conscious nuclear-free New Zealanders therefore had good reason to support Greenpeace and its protests against the French.

In a sense, the Rainbow Warrior was their flagship, and it had just been bombed in their own harbor (and it was New Zealand, after all, where a sheep getting away from the flock normally caused a hectic day). Their reaction to the bombing reminded me of the quiet neighbors at the end of my street, always nice until my BB went through their picture window. Not New York mad or Beirut mad. Politely mad in a proper sort of way, but infuriated, shocked, and outraged, nonetheless.

When an investigation did get underway, it didn't take Inspector Clouseau to figure out whodunit. The French commandos were caught with their wetsuits down. In the world opinion, France was already the bad guy for "nuking" the waters of the South Pacific. Now they were in hotter water for committing an act of terrorism. Ironically, the attack backfired on them in another way — sympathetic parties responded with massive monetary donations to Greenpeace.

The significance of the Rainbow Warrior's activity in the Pacific was deeper than most people realize. It was a political focal point for the young island countries of Oceania — nations that span across one-third of the Earth's surface. It was a region striving for true independence after two hundred years of being overrun by English, Spanish, French, Germans, Dutch, Portuguese, Japanese, New Zealanders, Australians, and Americans. Much of the original culture was churned through the mill of western imperialism (Hawaii and New Zealand, for example). Huge military bases were established over the region (Guam, Kwajalein, Truk, etc.). Some islands were ravaged for natural resources (such as phosphates), abandoned, and left with nothing (Palau, Kiribati). Others have been overwhelmed by twentieth century marketing, trade, and tourism (Tahiti, Fiji). Naturally, the island cultures that survived had a sense of self-preservation that made them resent being pawns of the first world nations. Greenpeace's anti-nuclear (anti-military, anti-imperialist) demonstrations were helping their collective voice be heard.

One of the anti-nuke issues Greenpeace was bringing to light was the history of the US military in the Marshall Islands. After the Second World War, the United States was appointed by the United Nations to oversee the Marshalls along with the other trust territories of Micronesia. The US was supposed to help them towards economic self-sufficiency and eventual independence. However, the US still keeps the region under its wing; the Federated States of Micronesia remains a UN trust territory today.

Shortly after the inception of the trust territories, the United States established atomic testing sites in the Marshalls and blasted them with a succession of 66 bombs. On March 1, 1954, radioactive fallout from a hydrogen bomb fell like snow on the island of Rongelap. The inhabitants lived on a three-inch deep radioactive "snowdrift" for three days before being evacuated. Within two weeks, their hair began falling out, and despite this indication, the US wouldn't admit to the severity of the problem. Three years later, they dumped the people back onto their island, claiming that it was again habitable. After thirty-one years of living with the effects of radiation-induced maladies including thyroid cancer, leukemia, still births, and miscarriages, the people of Rongelap were finally moved from their island. Their rescue ship was the Rainbow Warrior, on what was to be its last mission before setting sail for New Zealand.

The United States halted its activity in the Marshalls in 1958, and the rest of the world agreed to follow suit. However one country refused to limit its nuclear testing – France. In 1985, while the Rainbow Warrior was rescuing Marshallese radiation victims, the French detonated a 150 kiloton bomb in the Tuamotu Archipelago, their most powerful test to date. (As of this writing, they are still blasting the Tuamotus.)

მ& მ& მ&

13

In 1990, I found a job as an engineering geologist in Berkeley, California. This was paying the bills quite nicely, but work became incredibly dull every winter when the drillers and contractors shut down because of muddy conditions. I avoided this monotony by leaving in January '91 on a two month diving tour of New Zealand and the South Pacific.

When I arrived in Auckland, I thought it would be cool to do the Rainbow Warrior as my first wreck dive. (Back in '85, the wreckage of the Rainbow Warrior was becoming quite an eyesore, so the New Zealand government refloated it, towed it north to Cavalli Island, and scuttled it as a memorial.)

Across the channel from Cavalli Island, at Matauri Bay, I was directed to the only dive shop. The owner, a burly Maori named Dover, took customers out to the wreck when he wasn't trapping lobster or filling bags with abalone. I didn't have a wetsuit, so he loaned me his (water temperature = damn cold) and watched me carefully as I set up my gear. It was my first dive since Australia three years before, so I was struggling to remember what I'd learned. When he saw I was inexperienced, he jokingly nicknamed me Number One.

Dover's boat was typical for the region — overpowered. The monstrous outboard engine lifted the light hull until it seemed that only the propeller touched the water. Wind chop made the ride rough enough to knock out dental fillings.

"Slow down? You kidding me, Number One?"

When we finally arrived, Dover snagged the mooring buoy while I struggled on the bouncing deck to get my gear on. A tinge of seasickness began to lurk in my throat.

"Go straight down the line, Number One, and you'll find her."

I did a final check, spit in my mask, and back-rolled into the whitecaps. Finding the mooring line, I began my descent, relieved to be away from the nauseating motion. Below me, the bow of the ship came into view. The Rainbow Warrior sat upright on the flat bottom, 85 feet deep.

I headed towards the looming wheelhouse where the famous banner had hung. I paid my respects for a moment and then went

14

inside. (Before being scuttled, the ship had been stripped of dangling lines and other hazards to divers.) The walls of the dark rooms were barren, silently rusting into eternity. Fish hovered upside down below the ceiling, thinking it was actually the floor. I swam through the empty quarters where Fernando Pereira lost his life, poked around unsuccessfully for remnants, and then returned outside.

Brilliant colors couldn't penetrate to that depth, so I used my flashlight to show the reds, yellows, and purples of the sponges and hard corals. Orange and pink anemones made their home on the green paint of the hull. Other colorful organisms had also sprouted on the steel plating, decorating it brilliantly and appropriately — it had become a true sunken rainbow.

Back on the boat, Dover gave me an approving look. I had passed the initiation into his club. "Good dive, Number One?"

"Yeah. I feel kind of high, though. I think it's nitrogen narcosis."

He laughed. "You can't have narcosis on the surface, Number One."

"Oh. Well, I guess it's just from the thrill."

That night at a beach barbecue, we grilled fresh fish, abalone, and I tried a delicacy I'd never had — sea urchin roe, scraped from the inside of the shell and handed to me on the tip of Dover's knife. (It wasn't bad.) The next morning, I said farewell and headed back to Auckland for a flight to my next destination — Fiji.

TOMMY TALO
Fiji

"I like being hungover because it means I've done something that I absolutely love." Tommy

Fiji is famous for its striking color arrangements. Fish, sponges, and corals blend in brilliant reds that accent each other in a way that suggests a Claude Monet painting. After a short swim down the reef, the reds fade out and the effect is reproduced in greens, or pinks, or pastel purples — captivating all those lucky enough to be swimming by.

While planning my vacation, I visited a friend who had recently returned from a trip around the world. While looking through his photos, one in particular caught my eye. It was of a wild-haired man covered in white ash with his face charcoaled black around the eyes. He wore a grass skirt and held a spear menacingly as if guarding the grass hut on the beach behind him.

"Where's this? Africa?"

"Fiji"

"Really? Who's that guy?"

"That's me."

"You're kidding. How did you get dressed up like that?"

"That's what they do on this island where I stayed for three days."

"Wow. Could I go there?"

"Shouldn't be a problem. Let me show you where it is on the map."

His finger pointed to Waya, the largest island in the Yasawa Group.

I went to Fiji with Tommy (party animal *extraordinaire*) a couple years after we graduated from college. As soon as we arrived, we headed straight for the tourist information center.

17

Inside, behind the desk, an immense Fijian woman reclined half-asleep in a chair. She wasn't thrilled to see us, and when we asked about Waya, she muttered that it was not possible to visit an outer island without an invitation from a resident or special government permission. We didn't know anyone from the island so we asked how we could apply to the government. As she shut her eyes to resume her nap, she mentioned that even if we tried, permission would be virtually impossible to get. Heartbroken, we realized we had to plan a new vacation.

We checked into a hotel and dealt with the crisis by having a long cocktail session around the pool. When the afternoon sun began broiling the patio area, we moved into the water. Nearby, the bartender slumped onto a table, using his arm for a pillow. He muttered, "It's hot," to explain his behavior. I've heard that phrase in the islands over a thousand times since, but on that first afternoon, I thought, "Of course it's hot, you idiot, you live in the tropics." After awhile, I figured out that "It's hot" actually means "It's hotter than yesterday," or "It's hotter than this morning, and I'm just going to do absolutely nothing but sit in the shade until it's not hot."

(After a few years of living in the lesser latitudes, I have come to recognize that "hot" makes people sweat; anything cooler is just "warm." Interestingly, it often feels hotter in the evening when the temperature drops and the humidity subsequently rises. This is when your beer at sunset sweats more than you do, leaving a puddle on the table bigger than a dinner plate.)

That night, Tommy and I went to the Bamboo Palace nightclub, which was, as we found out, *the* place to be after hours. Being the only tourists inside, we were celebrities. Tommy was in full form, and as far as I can remember, so was I. We killed a lot of Fiji Bitters, cut the rug to the reggae band, and became friends with everyone in the place by the end of the night. The best sideshow was watching a burly young lady lose her temper with a taller skinnier woman on the dance floor. She leaned back and fired a haymaker into the girl's jaw, knocking her cold. The band kept playing as friends propped her in a chair and laid wet napkins on her head until she came to.

It didn't take long to find out that a lot of the other women had their sights set on us. Ebony beauties took turns planting their butts in our laps and whispering sweet nothings along the lines of, "Want to buy me a beer? You have a woman? Do you want one?" There was a lot of kissing going on by last call. Neither of us woke up alone.

Emerging hazily from our hotel into the blinding light of noon the next day, we were greeted warmly, "Hello, Tom. Hello, Mike. How are you today?"

"Fine. Thank you."

Both of us looked back, wondering when we had met.

Men and women alike continued to recognize us, "Hi, Mike! Hi, Tom!"

We'd say "Hi" back and then look at each other to see if either of us knew the person. Granted, it was a small town, but what had we *done*?

As we passed the tourist office, the woman who had ignored us the day before yelled, "Mike! Tom!" and came running out with a big smile. Her changed behavior wasn't the only surprise — we hadn't told her our names when we met.

"Do you still want to go to Waya?"

"Sure."

Without another word, she looked around, searching, until her gaze fell on a young woman on the opposite sidewalk. With a shout, she waved her over.

"That's Ruth. She's from Waya."

The girl dodged some traffic and came up to us. "Yes?"

"These gentlemen would like to go to Waya. Can you arrange it?"

She looked us over. "Yes. If you want, I can phone my cousin from your hotel and he can look after you when you go."

A few minutes later, she was in our lobby, calling the only phone on Waya. We waited as people searched the village for her cousin, and when he finally came to the phone, everything was arranged. His name was Sam Number Two and he would meet us the next day when the weekly supply boat arrived. What luck!

In the morning, Ruth picked us up and escorted us on the half-hour bus ride to Lautoka, the major port of Fiji's west coast. After spotting some Wayans waiting at the dock, she introduced us, said goodbye, and hopped on a bus going back. The village boat was a dilapidated tub that didn't look like it could cross the harbor, much less sail over the horizon. As every crate, barrel, box, or bale was loaded, the ship sank lower. Tommy muttered under his breath that we were on the SS Shark Food and that our doom was imminent. I told him to have faith. When the Wayans boarded, the boat was on the verge of foundering. Once underway, the bow wave pushed just enough water aside to keep it from flooding in over the gunwales.

The Wayans were hardly surprised by us. They had, after all, seen plenty of white people before. The predominant question was *why* we were there. Apparently, visitors were rare.

As the hills of Viti Levu faded behind us, a low form appeared on the horizon. Over the next four hours, the shape materialized into a lush island with bare volcanic cliffs leaping up from the water. We entered a bay, slowed as we crossed a reef, and landed on a long white beach. The village was nestled nearby under coconut palms and papaya trees.

Sam Number Two greeted us with a big smile. He was slim for a Fijian, and like the other men, wore only a sulu — a sarong style, cotton waist wrap. He walked with a noticeable limp because a few years earlier, a shark had taken a chunk out of his left calf while he was spearfishing. Since he'd almost died from the attack, he was put on island-style disability — meaning he didn't have to work, just wander around all day, sleep, and get fed. (This wasn't much different from what he would have being doing anyway because nobody in the village worked hard for more than a couple hours a day. Life is easy when the only required labor is to prepare meals, dig up some taro from the garden, do the washing, or spear a few fish.)

Sam led us through the village to his bure (boo-ray), the *Coconut Inn,* a raised wooden hut with no furniture, power, or running water. After showing us where to dump our packs, he took us to a nearby patch of sand that served as the family's "living room." His relatives, who lived in the adjacent bures, were waiting to meet us. Lani, his sister, seated us on a mat near the cooking area and served us fish, bananas, taro, and hot sweetened tea. Other villagers wandered by to meet us, including Sam's best friend, Russy. One man came in with a big smile and introduced himself as Sam Number One. At least that mystery was solved.

When Sam Number Two finished eating, he rinsed his hands in a finger bowl, rolled onto his back in the sand, and fell asleep in seconds. We didn't know what to do after our host deserted us, so Lani poured about seven more cups of tea while we chatted with her and Sam's father, Fish. After awhile, Sam sat up and wiped his eyes, but ignored the sand on his back.

Sam offered to take us to the beach, so we grabbed masks and snorkels and followed him to where the boat had pulled up. With his back still coated with sand, he angled toward a coconut palm and launched himself face-first into the shady spot at its base. This time, he rolled around to get comfortable and was soon fully adorned with every example of the regional geology.

After an hour on the reef, we returned to pick up Sam Number Two, who was awake and groggily staring at the tree. When we got back to the bure, Lani invited us to sit down and sip tea again; it became apparent that the list of guest activities was short. Sam took another nap, and our attention spans ran out. We asked if they had any beer. They didn't. Why? A few years before, on New Year's Eve, the drunken men had a brawl. A few were cut, and others were chased around the village. The infuriated chief subsequently banned every one of his subjects from booze for five years. What were we going to do for a week? Watching pineapples grow or estimating how fast sand would tumble off Sam's body wasn't going to do it for us.

After dinner, we found out what they did instead. Every night, the men got stoned on kava − ground or pounded pepper root prepared as a cold cloudy tea. That night, the kava fest was in the Coconut Inn. Russy was the grogmaster, preparing each batch by kneading a cotton cloth "tea bag" full of kava powder in a bowl of water. Sam Number Two, uncommonly animated, sat as close to the kava bowl as he could. This was the only time we saw him awake for more than three hours, and it became obvious that he was the most depraved of the dozen kava fiends in attendance. Russy gave us the option of having low tide (half-full cups) or high tide (full). I had no idea what effects to anticipate, so I eagerly gulped down high tides with the local boys. Tommy did the same.

(Kava contains a non-alcoholic drug that hits with a paralytic effect from the neck down. The brain remains fairly functional, but walking becomes difficult. To imagine what it feels like, think of the state of a tranquilized lion in the wild, helplessly glaring at a zoologist who is doing strange things to it with a thermometer. Kava drinking is still done in ceremonial silence as a coconut shell cup is passed around. Before receiving a drink, clap once. When finished, emphatically say "matha," pass the cup back to the "bartender," and clap three times in unison with everyone else. Clapping is done with cupped hands to produce a hollow pop, as opposed to a flat-handed smack. The drink is tossed back at once, shot style. Everyone shares the same coconut shell, and when the last person is finished, conversation resumes for twenty minutes or so until it is time for the next round.)

A mellow buzz crept up on me until I noticed that the kerosene lamp was emitting an uncommonly weird glow. Outside, only the wind, occasional distant laughter, and the chirps of geckos could be heard. As the grogfest continued, I was having trouble remembering Russy's name. After the next round, I tried to walk, but ended up careening wildly around as if walking on the deck of a ship in rough seas. After hanging off the side of the bure and wondering aloud why all the stars had changed positions, Russy cut me off and put me to bed. Tommy, on the other hand, appeared unfazed and carried on into the night with his new drinking buddies.

At dawn, someone started blowing a big horn, and the village erupted into life. On my mat inside the Coconut Inn, I could barely muster the energy to move, and I suddenly realized why Sam Number Two was listless all the time. I desperately wanted to go back to sleep, but the ensuing racket became hangover hell. The mayor went past every bure yelling something in Fijian that sounded like orders. Chicks were chirping loudly, roosters were crowing, and a cow was rubbing its head on the doorjamb. Babies were crying, pigs were making pig noises, and chickens were landing on the tin roof with a bang as if it were an aircraft carrier. To top things off, the flies were awake, and it was too hot to hide under a blanket. I had no choice but to get up.

As bad luck would have it, it was Sunday. As soon as I'd had my tea, Fish wrapped me in a sulu and headed me off towards the church. As we left, I spotted Tommy in the bure with his arms raised. Lani stooped next to him, wrapping him in a sulu so he could join me. He looked worse than I felt.

As guests of honor, the two of us were seated next to the altar. While the preacher droned, Tommy did the open-eyed asleep-on-the-feet trick that had gotten him through so many sermons as a child. As my own eyelids drooped, I dreamed of trussed missionaries stewing in huge cannibal cooking pots. What a price to pay for international relations. When we were finally released, we fled to join Sam Number Two for a nap on the beach.

The nightly grogfests continued in the same fashion, but toward the end of the week, we saw it done properly. The traditional kava welcoming, the most honored Fijian ritual, was held for some visiting guests. An hour before their arrival, the village make-up artists went to work on us with charcoal and ash while Lani located some traditional sulus. When they were finished, Tommy and I looked at each other's eyes blackened like the Lone Ranger's and broke out laughing. We stood out with our white skin and blonde hair, but what the hell, we had a party to go to.

The Fijians didn't look silly. They looked savage. Eyes peered coldly from behind ashen masks, and spears appeared in their hands. Their cannibal past was surfacing and nobody was smiling anymore. I was getting nervous.

It turned out that the "guests" were a dozen Australian tourists from a passing cruise ship. When they came ashore, Tommy and I waited quietly with the Fijian men. Our companions could have attacked and slaughtered the Aussies in minutes, but they remained calm as the guests approached. The tourists grinned nervously at the intimidating horde and seemed especially confused when they saw the two of us.

In front of us was a traditional "tanoa" (a three-foot-diameter hand-carved low wooden kava bowl on stubby legs) that was to function as the focal point of the activities. The Fijian women, wearing tamer ceremonial attire than the men, were seated beyond a fifty-foot open space in front of the bowl. The Australians stood to the side as their Fijian tour guide approached first and exchanged formalities with the master of ceremonies. He had a gunnysack filled with powdered kava as a gift (an appropriate offering as Waya's climate is too dry for it to grow). As everyone else maintained a required silence, the MC made a ritual speech and watched to make sure the mixer got the grog strength right in the tanoa. When the batch was ready, the mixer ran his hands around the rim of the tanoa and clapped out three deep thumps. Everyone was served a cup, and the ceremony ended.

That night, washed off and back to their relaxed habits, Sam Number One, Sam Number Two, Russy, Fish, and most of the other village men gathered in the village meeting house. I knew we were in for a marathon swill session when the same ceremonial tanoa was brought out and the gunnysack appeared. We were invited to sit with the mayor, a tall robust man who easily weighed 250 pounds. By ten o'clock, we were working on a pretty good buzz when word came down from the chief's house that all kava drinking had to be finished by midnight. Some huts needed to be repaired the next day, and the chief needed the men to be functional.

Hearing this, Tommy asked, "Hey, what do you guys say when you want another round?"

"We say Talo."

So Tommy responded immediately with "Talo," and another round was served.

As soon as it was finished, Tommy, Mr. All You Can Drink Before Closing Time, again proclaimed, "Talo."

There was a moment of stunned disbelief at this obvious breach of tradition, but nobody disagreed. Were they making an exception for us, or did the white boy just turn them on to a novel drinking concept?

"Talo . . . Talo . . . Talo . . . " Tommy, Mr. Non-Stop Binge, was in his element, spurring the former man-eaters on relentlessly.

After a few more rounds, some of the men rolled onto their backs, unable to sit up anymore. Next to the huge bulk of the mayor, Tommy looked tiny, and I'm sure everyone wondered how much more kava he could take. With every round, more men dropped out of the festivities. I was next, and the last thing I saw through my heavy-lidded lion eyes before I went to sleep was two remaining figures drinking on towards midnight. It was the mayor and Tommy. Everyone else was out cold.

The next morning, Tommy was still sleeping as I walked around. Instead of the familiar "Good Morning, Mike! How are you?" everyone said, "Hi, Mike. Where's Tom?"

The legend of Tommy Talo, new kava champion of Waya, had been born.

At lunch time, a special honor was bestowed on us. We were invited to the chief's house for a private kava session. I guessed he had to see this blue-eyed phenomenon for himself. We didn't know if it would be a good idea to get the chief hammered, so we were glad when the meeting turned out more formal than wild. We were limited to three, had a conversation filled with mutual compliments, and supported the local economy by purchasing a few postcards of the village.

At the end of the week, Sam Number Two and Russy went with us back to Lautoka. Desperate for something besides taro, We marched them straight to the nearest hamburger restaurant.

As the waitress set down two cold pints of draught Fiji Bitter in front of us, Sam and Russy eyed the mugs.

Nobody else from Waya was around, so Tommy and I nodded to each other. "We won't tell anybody if you want to join us."

They stared back like we just didn't get it. We didn't. We had no idea that traditional chiefs were so powerful. The faithful subjects across from us wouldn't think of touching a beer. A decree from the chief banning alcohol meant No Drinking. Words to Moses couldn't have been any clearer.

After seeing them off on the SS Shark Food's return trip, we checked into our hotel, found sanctuary around the pool, and took a brief vacation from our Fijian vacation. After completing our rejuvenation with a steak dinner, we wandered over to the Bamboo Palace and were greeted with a chorus of, "Hey, Tom and Mike are back!" We were still famous for God knows what the previous week, but we never could remember enough from the first night to figure out what it was.

ABENTEUER
Tonga

"An adventure is never fun while it's happening." Ken

To get to the limestone islands of Vava'u from Tonga's capital, Nuku'alofa, I took the government night ferry, a rusty old tub, that, for reasons nobody seemed to understand, sailed with a permanent thirty degree list to starboard. I spent a hellish night outside on a bouncing deck crowded with seasick Tongans.

Grateful when it finally pulled into Neiafu, the central town of the Vava'u Group, I jumped ashore to look for the only dive shop, which I'd heard was run by an American. What I found was an unlocked, unoccupied, weathered aluminum shed. A few tanks and a gasoline powered compressor lay in disarray on the floor. Hung on the wall were tattered photocopies of the Yank's diplomas: an engineering degree from the University of Washington and two more from the Massachusetts Institute of Technology. Unfortunately, he was off-island, and I never found out what he was doing there. So much for diving.

There was a German named Rainer at the guesthouse whose English wasn't very good, so using my college German, I invited him along on a trip to Mariner's Cave, a sealed chamber on an island ten miles to the south. To get there, we rented the island's only functional sailboat, a battered looking Hobie Cat with a canvas tarp between the twin hulls just big enough for the two of us. After getting directions and a crude map, we sailed out of the harbor across Faihava channel to the island of Nuapapu. When we neared the cave's landmarks, I jumped in with a mask to look for the entrance and found myself in the clearest water I'd ever seen. A hundred feet of visibility is considered to be excellent by everyone. Two hundred is even fantastic for the hardest of old timers. Three hundred feet away, a school of surgeonfish prodded the sand looking for food, seemingly ant-sized at that distance. I spotted the entrance easily and tied the Hobie to a coral head.

The cave opening was an oblong hole a body length below the surface. We entered by taking a deep breath, diving down, and swimming through the tunnel for ten full seconds. When the passage opened up, we turned upward and surfaced in the inner chamber, a cave the size of a three-car garage. Light leaked in through a gash in the rock twenty feet below the entrance, dimly illuminating the drab limestone walls. The water level rose and fell in a cycle that started with the muffled thump of a wave smacking the cliff outside. As water rushed in below, we were launched towards the ceiling. A few feet short of impact, we slowed to a stop, then dropped away. Since the chamber was sealed, the air inside was at its maximum humidity. Whenever the water level fell, the air pressure dropped, causing a thick fog to form. With every upsurge, the pressure increased, restoring clarity.

After twenty marvelous minutes, we swam back out. I untied the Hobie, secured our gear bag to the mast, and sailed for home. The wind picked up, and the boat bounced hard across the small whitecaps. Then, when we hit the rougher waves in the channel, everything went to hell. A loud pop exploded from the port hull, and within seconds, it flooded and sank, capsizing the boat. The mast hit the water as Rainer and I were thrown overboard.

We quickly grabbed onto the floating starboard hull and looked around in vain for any boats or people in sight. The closest land was the southwestern tip of Vava'u, over a mile away to the north. To make things worse, a strong current was rushing us westward into open ocean. Even with fins on, it was doubtful that we could swim to Vava'u before being swept out to sea. The prospect of waiting for the Tongan Navy to find us while we died of thirst or were eaten by sharks in the middle of the Pacific had us thinking fast.

Rainer didn't know how to sail, so I coached him through a desperate plan. I had him pull on the mainstay while I stood on the hull and levered back on the halyard. After minutes of fighting the weight of the soaked sail, we managed to get the mast up in the air. I found that if I hung from the halyard over the water, I could counterbalance the flooded hull. If Rainer tried to board, his weight would cause another capsize so he had to hang onto the hull near my feet while I worked with the rigging. After a few minutes of careful maneuvering, I was able to get the sail to fill. I wondered if we were moving and then noticed tiny eddies behind the rudders. Thank God, but could we make it in time? Rainer hugged the hull tightly with his arms and legs as waves broke over his back. There was no way to steer the sunken hull into the wind, so returning to the harbor was impossible. As the current took us further west, I "pointed up" into the wind to keep the last bit of land ahead of us, hindering our minuscule pace even more.

Rainer's voice came up out of the splashing turmoil at my feet. "Koennen wir es?"

"Ja. We can do it."

As soon as I uttered that reassuring statement, a blast of wind knocked the boat over, launching me back into the water.

"Scheisse!"

We scrambled furiously to get it back up and into position. Crucial minutes had been lost. Up and running again, I saw how far the land had moved sideways and realized that the current was a virtual torrent. As minutes passed, the tip of the island slipped away to windward as I struggled furiously to aim the boat towards it. We weren't going to make it. Real terror was building as I struggled to think of a new plan. Then, I noticed shapes in the water. It was a reef! I let out a shout and pointed for Rainer to look. He couldn't see a thing with the waves smacking his face, but he figured it out thirty seconds later when his feet plopped down on coral. I jumped in to join him and we started wading against the current towards a beach, dragging the pathetic Hobie behind us. In knee deep water we stopped and looked back at the endless stretch of open ocean. Rainer's comment? "Abenteuer!" (Adventure!) He was definitely a man of few words.

When we got the Hobie ashore, we drained it, dragged it up the sand, and tied it to a tree. Fortunately, the small village of Longomapu was less than a mile away. The villagers there stared at us as if we had just wandered out of a Jules Verne novel, but didn't mind when we invited ourselves into the back of a truck that was leaving for Neiafu, twenty miles away on dirt roads. Three hours later, we tromped through the doorway of the guesthouse and found the angry owner of the Hobie waiting for us. He didn't know that we had left the harbor, so when we told him his boat was shipwrecked off Longomapu, he started yelling and hopping around like the Tasmanian Devil. We countered by blaming him for renting us a defective boat. It eventually ended in a stalemate.

ॐ ॐ ॐ

I was told that the American's divemaster, Nili, could arrange a two-tank dive for the next day. Rainer wasn't a diver, so Nili and I went alone. The first dive penetrated a labyrinth of darkened tunnels underneath a limestone island named Kitu. Deep inside, on the sandy floor of a tiny cave, a dozen whitetip reef sharks slept in seclusion.

The second dive was Aa Wall, a vertical bank of coral alongside one of the islands that Rainer and I had drifted away from during our epic. Nili showed off by harassing black durgeons, a type of triggerfish. (Triggerfish range from thumbnail size to a foot-long and are noted for two things: triggers, and powerful jaws. The triggers are hard cartilage spikes that hinge out of the tops of their heads along with a lesser defined trigger behind their lower jaws. When threatened, the fish dart into the nearest hole and throw their triggers apart, making it impossible to be dragged out by a predator. Triggers, pound for pound, are the most ferocious biters in the ocean. When they attack smaller fish, they often cut them cleanly in half with surprisingly loud lightning-quick chomps.) Nili's trick was to chase a durgeon into a small hole and let it lock in with its "triggers." Reaching in with a finger, we were able to pet its tail while it audibly "clucked" its disapproval at us. We were careful not to reach into larger holes, knowing the fish could turn and nip hunks out of our fingers.

Lionfish, one of the most beautiful species on the reef, have red-striped frilly fins that hide poisonous spines. They pose haughtily like peacocks, and are unafraid of predators. Their cumbersome appearance makes them look slow, but they can drop their ornamentation flat and accelerate instantly. At the base of Aa wall, a small wrasse was careless enough to turn its back on a lionfish six feet in the distance. The lionfish seemed to vanish and then reappear where the wrasse had been. The smaller fish had been swallowed whole in a split second.

Our third dive was Swallow's Cave, a domed cavern with a fern shrouded entrance that faced west. Underneath, the rays of the setting sun formed a fifty-foot golden shaft of light in the water, spotlighting a circle on the sandy bottom. Waves moved by, breaking the angled beam into dancing lines of light. Hovering on scuba in the middle of all that, I felt I had gone to heaven. The only thing missing was an underwater Walkman playing The Dark Side of the Moon.

ã€€ã€€ ã€€ã€€ ã€€ã€€

Eventually it was time to leave Vava'u. I couldn't brave the ferry again, so I booked a ticket with Friendly Island Airways, my final Tongan adventure.

"What time is the flight?" I asked the clerk.

"Just head out to the airstrip around noon and wait until you hear the plane coming."

Alone at the one shack terminal, I waited for an hour. No plane. I got bored, collected a couple coconuts, opened them on a stake, and ate them. Around one, a pick-up truck with three guys wearing Friendly Islands Airways shirts showed up. They wandered in, took my ticket, and impressed me by producing luggage destination tags. My bag was then placed in the designated outgoing baggage spot, an unmarked patch of asphalt next to the doorway. We played checkers for another hour before hearing the sound of an approaching turboprop.

My checkers partner said, "Here comes your flight."

"Oh, really?" I thought.

A twin engine Otter with "Friendly Islands" painted on the side came bouncing down the turf. The ground crew notified me that the flight had arrived, and that I could now board. They shoved my bag through a hatch in the nose and directed me up a stepladder into the cramped cabin. The pilot was dressed nicely and seemed sober, so I scrambled in and sat behind him. It's always reassuring to fly with an airline that can't afford to crash.

The flight itself was routine and in good weather all the way. As we sighted Fuaamotu International Airport, I wondered why the pilot didn't go into an approach pattern for the runway. My question was answered when he landed on the grass next to the terminal instead.

I was back in civilization, almost.

THE HEART OF POLYNESIA
Western Samoa

"Travel is the frivolous part of serious lives and the serious part of frivolous ones." Mme. Swetchine

Samoa! At last, the most unspoiled Pacific culture. Following in the footsteps of Margaret Mead, Somerset Maugham, and Robert Louis Stevenson, I set out to discover what the legends were all about. Apia, the capital, is where the flights land. It is a sleepy harbor town on the island of Upolu, which is a rough rectangle to the southeast of the nation's other isle, volcanic Savai'i. (Interestingly, Savai'i and Hawai'i have identical meanings in their respective Polynesian dialects — sacred homeland.) Both of these Samoan islands are densely foliated, coral ringed, and beautiful. Many waterfalls adorn high volcanic cliffs as feathery white cascades.

Multicolored buses, kept shiny with daily cleanings, dot the roads in contrast to the uniform backdrop of rural green. Fenders may be painted sky blue, hoods may be red, grills green, bumpers white, and so on. Inside, the scheme is equally vivid. Window tassels flutter back and forth with every bounce down dusty potholed roads. Caged chickens, tied pigs, and bales of pandanus are regularly carted in and out through the rear door at obscure undetermined stops.

With plans to circle the island, I hailed one of these coaches and stumbled back to an empty seat as it jostled around. Speakers mounted in the corners belted "Ice Ice Baby," a popular hit at the time — and one I would hear no less than seven more times before I disembarked. The woman that I sat next to was all smiles, and when we reached her village, she invited me into her home. As I was going to find out, this was a common

Samoan gesture towards visitors. As the bus pulled away, the sounds of "Under the Boardwalk" faded into silence.

The village appeared to be very traditional, except for the presence of a small church. As Tili and I walked down the road, small children spotted me and rushed up shouting, "Palangi! Palangi!" (Foreigner! Foreigner!). People smiled and waved from their houses, many gesturing for me to join them, but I was already taken.

The houses were fales (fah-lays), huts with raised wooden floors, thatched roofs, but no walls (it was considered rude to hide behind "closed doors"). That didn't allow for much privacy, but in a village that small, everyone knew what everyone else was doing anyway. There was one fale for each married couple, and they shared it with unmarried family members. At Tili's fale, I was given the best mattress, best sleeping space, and the first serving of food at mealtimes, despite my respectful insistence not to be spoiled. As I ate, my plate was fanned constantly by a woman or child to keep the flies off. Nobody else would start eating until I was finished.

As the honored guest of a home in the village, I was invited for tea at the preacher's house. It was hot sitting around with no wind, so his seventeen-year-old daughter peeled off her T-shirt. My discretion was put to the ultimate test, but I couldn't resist a glance at her young brown breasts. The preacher told her to put her shirt back on.

After hearing that I was a geologist, he brought out a small metallic rock that had been found in the jungle and asked me to identify it. I didn't have a clue what it was so I chipped off a piece and later took it back to California. Everyone I worked with in the office was stumped, so we had it X-rayed in a spectrograph. It was elemental silicon, a mineral not known to occur naturally. The mystery remains. Was this a rare fluke caused by some intense volcanic heat under perfect circumstances? Was it a piece of a satellite that burned up on re-entry and landed in Samoa? Did somebody dump it there? Did it actually get found in the jungle? I'll never find out without going back and launching a full investigation.

Seeing the preacher as a non-traditional leader in the village reminded me that Christian missionaries had overwhelmed these people with technology, wealth, a written language, and of course, the wrath of God. On Sunday, the villagers gathered devoutly in church and sang hymns in magnificent harmonies that angels couldn't possibly have ignored, but as soon as the service was over, everything reverted to the way it was before the church was built. (One thing the missionaries didn't conquer was sexual promiscuity. There are only two things to do out there, and one of them is fishing.)

Streams are the freshwater sources in the villages. They are also used for bathing, washing, and cooling off when it gets too hot. Near the village was a swimming hole at the mouth of a lava tube, a natural tunnel formed by an ancient underground river of magma. It headed off deep into the earth towards the site of the former volcano. Inside were a few chambers with air pockets that could be reached by snorkeling down through holes and coming up on the other side. Feeling adventurous, I took a dive light and explored the pitch blackness. In the back of the farthest chamber, I dove through an opening, but couldn't see an air pocket, so I backed out.

I swam back out to where the other people were sitting and asked, "Excuse me, do you know if there is a cave behind the one through there?"

A teenage boy nodded. "Yes, there is."

"Thanks."

After returning to the back of the cave, I hyperventilated a few times and relaxed to extend my breath-hold time. I dove down, swam all the way through, and looked for the air pocket. There was none. I turned to go back but the entrance hole was obscured by silt stirred up from my fin wash. Being unable to see scared the hell out of me, which made me desperate to breathe. I found the hole and swam through, continuing as far as I could to make sure I cleared it, and came up in the main cave completely out of breath. I couldn't believe how stupid I had been. I was in the back chamber for a minute or more. In another twenty seconds, I would have drowned. Then I realized what I had overlooked in my question to the boy. I should have asked if there was *air* in the cave.

The women in the village used knives to open cans, so on my way home from the cave, I thought it would be nice to get a proper can opener for Tili and her family. When I presented it, she thanked me and laid it on a shelf as if putting it on display. Special gifts aren't for everyday use, apparently; they stuck with the knife method afterward. Oh well, the thought was there.

I finally bade farewell to my adopted family and continued my journey. There wasn't any traffic, so by late afternoon I had walked around the entire eastern end of the country. When a pickup truck finally came by, the driver had me squeeze in front next to his wife rather than sit in back with the others. They were eventually headed across the middle of the island to Apia, but I wanted to stay on the coast and circumnavigate the island. When we got to the turnoff, I asked to be let out.

"Here?" they asked.

"Sure. Why not?"

"It's going to be dark soon."

"That's okay. If I can't get a ride tonight, I'll camp."

"How can you camp?"

"I've got a hammock and some food and water."

They spoke with each other in Samoan for a moment.

"We can't let you do that."

"It's okay. I camp all the time. It's no problem for me."

"No we can't allow you. It is too dangerous."

"Because of thieves?"

"No. Spirits."

"Spirits?"

"And witches. They are very bad here."

I couldn't argue with that, so they insisted on driving me down the coast road to their cousin's house. It was a half-hour out of their way, and the cousins had no idea I was coming. We pulled up in the dark and my situation was explained. Once again, I was spoiled by awesome hospitality.

In the morning, I was invited along on a spearfishing trip to their family island, Nu'usafe'e. I hopped in a little outrigger and

36

paddled out behind the two teenage sons. When we got there, we hit the water armed with Hawaiian slings (spears shot slingshot style, rather than from a spear gun). As soon as I got my mask cleared, I was greeted by a fantastic display. As far as I could see, table corals grew up through each other like crowded mushrooms, forming an interlaced carpet of delicate tiered formations.

After shooting a dozen fish, we went to the beach. The boys immediately dug their fingers into the fish bellies and started pulling out select organs to munch on. They ate the eyes, also.

"Have some, Mike."

"That's okay, guys. I'll hold out for the barbecue."

THE SEASICK DIVEMASTER
Monterey, California

"He's Jimmy, the seasick man,
Throwing up raisin bran,
The fish want to meet him,
And we'll gladly leave him,
He's Jimmy, the seasick man, toot toot." (Keep reading)

After two months of working two nights a week and weekends for my divemaster internship, I was finally getting certified as a professional diver — my passport to the world. I could now travel anywhere and work. Since Jimmy and I were completing our divemaster courses at the same time, we carpooled from Berkeley to Monterey for our last required dives. Jimmy was allowed a space for his sleeping bag on the instructors' hotel room floor. I had access to the fold-out couch in my buddy Big Al's small apartment.

Big Al was a mischievous Italian New Yorker, known to his friends as an unscrupulous womanizer and the root of all evil. He was stationed at Fort Ord at the time, flying helicopters for the Army. I had witnessed his best night moves at a beer joint called Doc Rickett's Lab, a basement bar in Monterey with live music, dancing, and pool tables. We were shooting a game down there one night when a young unaccompanied lady started watching. Al went over and chatted her up for less than a minute, then came back to the pool table. A while later, two young Swedish men came in, hit on her, and started buying her drinks at the bar.

"Al, what's the scoop?"

He looked at me as if I had lost my faith. "Relax, Z. It's under control."

Later, when we headed for the door, Al paused at the bar to whisper a word in the woman's ear. She thanked the Swedish guys for the drinks, put her arm around Al and left with us.

The next morning, after he took her home, I asked, "Al, what did you say to her last night? Whatever it was, it's got to be the greatest line in history."

"Trade secret."

"Al, I got to know."

"Baby, I want your Scooby snacks on my face."

"Come on, Al, that wasn't it. Be serious."

He never told.

Unlike Al, Jimmy was a baby faced kid, freshly discharged from the Army after Desert Storm. When I introduced them at Doc Rickett's on Saturday night, I feared that I might be handing a lamb to a wolf. Al knew we weren't diving until ten the next morning, so he didn't hold back when it came to ordering rounds.

After a couple games of pool, I came back from the toilet to find Al explaining the rules of liar's poker to Jimmy. I butted in to scold Al, "No. No. No." I draw the line when he tries to hustle my friends. Liar's poker, for those who are naive to the trick, is a simple bluffing game using the digits in the serial numbers of dollar bills. For example: three ones beats two ones, and four eights beats three nines. Eventually it gets to the point where someone has to lie to beat the other and hope they don't get discovered. Getting caught lying means losing. It seems like a fair game until you realize that Al's wallet is loaded with his favorite bills, all full of nines.

Jimmy went back to his beer and Al found a liar's poker sucker at the next table. After losing a few times, the guy said, "Hey something's fishy here. Let's trade bills before we play this next one." He handed over a bill he hadn't looked at for one Al had memorized. Some people are destined losers.

That's when Jimmy made his fatal mistake; he revealed that it was his twenty-first birthday. Now we had true reason to celebrate, and Al was merciless.

"Hey Jimmy, how ya doin' there, buddy? Ever had a B-52?"

We walked down the street to a nightclub only to find a huge line at the door. Al said, "Follow me and do what I do." He led us into the men's room and pulled up short. "It's really busy and this is the only bathroom. When we come out, the bouncers will think we've already been in." After waiting three minutes, we strode out with our best poker faces. The bouncers waved us past the $7 COVER sign like they knew us. Inside, Al let out his satanic victory chuckle and grabbed a table. I was starting to worry about Jimmy; he had a carefree smile and wasn't walking very straight.

The band was rocking, and Al tried to get Jimmy out on the dance floor.

"Hey, come on, buddy. There are some cuties out there."

"Nah, I can't"

"Howzya drink doin' then? Want another one?"

Jimmy listed on his chair. When the band did a great rendition of Van Halen's "Eruption," Jimmy jumped up without a word and ran out, fleeing for his life.

When I got up the next morning, a hammer was rhythmically beating the hell out of the back of my forehead. I rummaged through Al's medicine chest until I found aspirin and Visine. After nabbing a roll of breath mints from a drawer, I headed straight out for a giant coffee and a Sausage McMuffin. With that in my system, I would be able to show up intact at the wharf.

As I walked up the gangplank, my instructor glowered at me. "Thanks a lot, Mike."

"For what?"

"For getting Jimmy *hammered*."

I gave him the Big Al "who me?" shrug.

"Jimmy staggered in last night and lost his dinner all over our bathroom along with whatever else you poured into him."

Like I had many times in the past, I was left shouldering the blame for the devil himself.

On the boat, Jimmy was looking rough. After casting off the lines and signing the divers in, we went up to the foredeck.

When the boat left the harbor and hit the slow Pacific swells, I started feeling queasy.

"Oh, I can feel it. We shouldn't have had so much to drink last night."

Jimmy, graying, only nodded yes.

A moment later, I heard what sounded like a big hiccup from him. I looked upwind and saw his cheeks puffed out like a squirrel's.

"Are you gonna . . . ?"

He nodded yes again.

I was in the worst possible place, so I vaulted up over the rail onto the bridge. Jimmy did a "Chips Ahoy," blowing cookies into the briny blue. Afterward, he staggered back through the twenty or so customers and splayed himself over the transom.

Seasickness shows a complete absence of mariners' favorite pride — sea legs. Real sailors don't barf. Divemasters count as crew and are therefore subject to this age old law of the sea. Watching Jimmy leaning over the rail, one of the instructors burst into song with new lyrics to Popeye the Sailor Man. Fortunately, Jimmy couldn't hear any of it over the clamor of the exhaust ports. Each instructor, in turn, devoted a new verse to him until they were laughing too hard to continue. People express themselves strangely after their bathroom gets wiped out.

SHIPWRECKED
Truk/Palau

"Wreck dive? I thought you were the wreck." Smart-ass
customer

February, 1992

TRUK

Back in California, I researched dive magazines and
National Geographics, looking for a location for the ultimate
wreck diving trip. Truk lagoon became the obvious choice
because of its warm water and the eighty ships sunk there by
American aircraft in February, 1944. As a kid, I sat for hours in
front of Victory at Sea TV shows. Now, I lined the walls of my
office with wreck photos and ship silhouettes labeled with
names like Aikoku, Kiyosumi, and Gosei. My dreams involved
languid exploration through passageways where sailors once
walked. When the work season slowed at the end of the year, I
bought a ticket that took me through all the regional centers of
Micronesia, including Truk and Palau.

In Truk, I met up with Bill, a fellow geologist I worked with
in Berkeley. We were obsessed with the idea of poring over the
cargo holds and discovering gas masks, guns, and teacups, but
by the time we left, we had seen so many of those common
items, we hardly noticed them. Instead we raved about
periscopes, torpedoes, binoculars, typewriters, phonographs,
surgical instruments, candlesticks, fans, wheelbarrows, rubber
galoshes, artillery pieces, airplanes, tanks, trucks, steamrollers,
bicycles, motorcycles, bathtubs, and Asian style squat toilets.
Spent bullet shells, fired during the battle, still existed in good
condition, dented primers and all.

43

The most common war wrecks were Japanese armed freighters and tankers. They were designated by the word "Maru," meaning "non-war ship." These ships varied from moderate to massive in size, most of them longer than a football field. All of them had a large-bore revolving gun mounted atop the forecastle. Open cargo holds or baffled oil compartments stretched back to the bridge superstructure. Behind the bridge was another hold and the engine room. The stern was armed with a second cannon and anti-submarine depth charge throwers on the fantail. Since the keel was the densest point on the ships, most settled in upright positions as they sank. Some, however, flipped upside down or landed at wild angles. Freighters had high "goal post" style masts straddling the holds for loading. Many of these are still intact today and are handy references for finding upright wrecks.

The local crews were amazingly good at finding deep wrecks in the vast lagoon. They lined up marks on distant islands, then threw non-damaging wheel-rim anchors overboard. The captain would confidently declare something like, "Stern gun," and sure enough, when we got down there, we'd find the line draped over the barrel of a stern gun.

Most of the shipwrecks in Truk were over a hundred feet deep, which limited our dive times to twenty or thirty minutes maximum. It would be easy for us to "squander" a dive by wandering the decks aimlessly, so Bill and I used dive computers and a carefully thought out dive plan to maximize our bottom time. After coaxing one of the local guides into actually working, we got him to take us to the highlights on each ship, then left him and headed straight for the engine rooms. Dark and hidden below the deck, they offered a fresh world that hadn't been combed over by the average dive tourist. Amidst the massive steel hulks of the engines which, on older ships, included boilers with coal chutes, we found light bulbs dangling in their sockets, console gauges, and speaking tubes. When I saw a glass thermometer protruding from a boiler, I signaled Bill over with my light. I dusted the thin coating of muck off and read it at 29 degrees Celsius, still accurate after a half-century in the drink.

৵ ৵ ৵

Night diving is a great way to see how the other half lives while the daytime inhabitants of the reef snooze. Flashlight beams dart through the black water as divers look around, an odd visual effect that spills over to other senses. Familiar dive sites by day become mysterious enveloping mediums. Crabs, shrimp, and lobster come out from reef crevices to feed, and shells emerge from the sand to scoot around at surprisingly quick speeds. Glow-in-the-dark worms leave trails in the water and plankton glow green when disturbed. Squid and cuttlefish freeze in the beam of a light and can be touched. Many of the fish sleeping in holes change to duller colors at night. Parrotfish go so far as to create a transparent "mucus cocoon" around themselves for protection.

On the Shinkoku Maru, Bill and I started our night dive early and watched the wreck "bloom" before our eyes. As dusk became darkness, nocturnal coral polyps emerged from their hard skeletal casings to feed, adding brilliant color to the drab iron hulk. Inside the engine room we found a catwalk thirty feet above the floor. The crystal clear water seemed to be air, a dramatic effect emphasized by the point source lighting in our hands. As a goof, I jumped off headfirst and fell to the floor below in a slow motion swan dive. Bill watched and did the same. The illusion of flying through air was a major trip. We ended up side by side between the boilers, 110 feet below the surface.

৵ ৵ ৵

Six days later, after leaving the engine room on the Kensho Maru, we "stumbled" through a companionway into the galley. There were woks on the stove, utensils hanging on the wall, and platters and pans on the shelves — as if the cook had

45

just stepped out for a cigarette. Against the corner juncture of the bulkhead and ceiling, a pocket of trapped scuba bubbles glittered. After poking our hands up into it, we found it had enough room for our heads. Careful not to inhale air that was possibly contaminated, we took breaths on our regulators before removing them. Our voices, compressed by the pressure, sounded as if our ears were clogged.

On the Unkai Maru #6, while sifting through the muck with my fingers, I hit a hard object and pulled out a book. All other paper on board had decomposed years before, but this had been protected by the sludge. Opening it, I found beautiful Japanese script printed on delicate pages in blue ink. After taking a good look, I gingerly re-buried it.

We were entering wreck overload mode. All of our experiences were dissolving into a homogenous clump in our memories. After two forty-minute dives, we sat around with our logbooks, struggling to remember anything we had seen. We asked around and found that this was a common experience among the divers who dove deeper than 100 feet. One theory is that the high carbon-dioxide concentration at depth impairs the brain's ability to remember.

ॐ ॐ ॐ

The islands of the Truk lagoon are each small enough to be explored in a day. The fortified defenses left by the Japanese are still intact, though some are overgrown. Bunkers with bomb holes and protruding cannon barrels can be found in strategic positions overlooking the former anchorage. With a map, they can be easily reached on foot, though it is imperative that you ask permission from the property owners before visiting the sites. It is also necessary to be armed with a couple baseball-sized rocks to fend off territorial mutts.

For evening entertainment, Bill and I played speed chess with a clock at the hotel restaurant. I tried flirting with one of the waitresses and found out how efficient the coconut telegraph can be. Ten minutes later, a man came in through the front door, walked straight up to our table, and invited himself to sit down.

After a few minutes of small talk, he bluntly stated, "I'm her brother."

I took that to mean "Hands off."

Other than that, the only exciting thing happening was an excellent Japanese restaurant near the Intercontinental Hotel, where I kept the chefs working full time – "maguro, ebi, and more wasabi, *please!*"

℞ ℞ ℞

PALAU

I didn't know that air strikes on Palau occurred just after the attack on Truk, so I was surprised to find war wrecks there as well.

Every now and then a "new" wreck is found, such as the Helmet Wreck, which lay undiscovered for over forty-five years in the harbor. We were among the first to dive it. The holds were full of rifles, machine guns, lanterns, gas masks, china, radios, and stacks of steel army helmets. Rifle ammunition was on the aft deck which indicated that at least one sailor was shooting at the American planes with a 6.5 millimeter rifle. Down in the forward hold were uniforms, crates of antiaircraft ammo, and medicine bottles with medicine still inside of them. Unfortunately, no one can find any of this stuff today because of pilfering.

I am a strong advocate of leaving artifacts intact on wrecks. These ships are underwater museums and should be respected as such. The Helmet Wreck today is a perfect example of why. The only things left on this wreck are objects too big to be slipped into a diver's pocket. Who is benefiting from this? If these items had resale value, I could understand why people would steal them, but they don't and end up gathering dust on a private shelf where few can enjoy them.

The Iro Maru, an armed freighter, is the best Palauan wreck. Although a popular site, its true secrets have been untouched by pilferers because of its huge size, hidden holds, and 120 foot bottom depth. A dozen dives are needed to fully explore it. The first is usually spent getting a feel for the ship's layout and checking out the guns and black coral on the deck. Three more dives are needed to get acquainted with the ship's interior. Then adventurous divers can concentrate on isolated sections.

Unlike most ships, the Iro didn't have open holds. There were three tiers of cargo space instead. Deep in the stern, we found wooden crates with gas masks in perfect condition. Their rubber hoses were still coiled up, last touched by workers in Japan.

The Japanese loved baths, and tubs are found throughout the ship. They also loved beer. Deep in the forward hold are ten cases of untouched "Nippon Brewing Co. Ltd." bottles. The brewery name is embossed in the glass, but unfortunately, the caps have rusted off. We also found bottles bearing the name "Sakura (cherry blossom) Beer."

The rusted-out captain's quarters must have been lavish before the Iro went under. It had an adjoining head with a porcelain sit-down toilet, sink, and bathtub. Under one of the two beds was a heater for cold nights.

ə ə ə

At the tip of Ngargol Island, pillboxes concealed inside the limestone cliffs guarded the harbor entrance. Scott, the other divemaster, dropped Bill and me off on the rocky shore, and waited while we crawled inside to investigate the rusted machine guns. When we came out, we stumbled across a five-foot banded sea snake recuperating from a boat propeller cut. Bill loved reptiles and was a trained snake handler, but when he reached down to grab it, I felt I had to warn him.

"Hey, watch it. Those things are deadly poisonous."

He scoffed at me and picked up the snake from behind the head. I figured he knew what he was doing.

Scott looked over from the boat and yelled, "Hey, don't you know those things are more deadly than a cobra?"

Bill's jaw dropped. Apparently, he thought I was kidding. I wished I had a camera to capture his expression as he gingerly set it back down.

THE RAPTURE OF THE DEEP
Vanuatu / Truk / Palau

"By then, we were about two hundred fifty feet beneath the surface, and I could see, stretching temptingly below me, as far as my eyes could reach, what seemed the infinite sweetness and quiet of a blackness that would yield up the secrets of the universe if only I were to go a bit deeper . . . " Jacques

By rapture, I don't mean staring at Swedish women diving in their bikinis. I am talking about the three-martini buzz of nitrogen narcosis, a phenomenon that hits everyone in one way or another at depths of a hundred feet or more. It sets in immediately, sometimes as shallow as eighty feet and influences the diver more greatly as he goes deeper. The effects lessen whenever the diver moves into shallower water and disappear near the depth where they appeared.

The usual symptom is a peaceful and happy euphoria. Time and space are disoriented in a fashion similar to the numbing effects of a high fever. Attention wanders aimlessly, and the imagination may offer unrealistic suggestions. Narcosis varies unpredictably from dive to dive. For example, a diver may go to 120 feet in the morning and be high as a kite. Returning to the same location in the afternoon, he may feel normal. Reaction time and judgment may be impaired, but this often goes unnoticed. Increased anxiety is also a symptom, and it can sometimes push divers to the brink of panic. Narcosis itself is not harmful, but a "narced" diver's behavior can be. Unlike the hazards of mountain climbing, the dangers of the deep are not naturally recognized by the brain. Some narced divers have lost their judgment and continued into the depths, but were either stopped by their buddy or the bottom. Others never made it back.

51

My first encounter with it was in Vila Bay, Vanuatu, on the Star of Russia. The wreck sat upright on the flat harbor bottom, 120 feet deep. The divemaster gave us a bottom time of fifteen minutes, followed by a three minute stop at twenty feet and a four minute stop at ten. After a minute-long descent down a mooring line that seemed to drop into oblivion, the rotted remains of the old clipper emerged, sprawling before us like the ribcage of a hulking skeleton on the muddy harbor bottom. The wood had rotted away, leaving upright metal supports. Lined-up like the sides of a clamshell, they beckoned us to their embrace. The only fish in sight hovered near the bow. Narcosis tranquilized my nervousness and caused time to crawl. The eerie two-hundred-foot ship seemed to be hundreds of yards long as we swam its length. The water seemed thick. I felt that I was barely moving, weak, and finning helplessly in my dream state. In this condition, fifteen minutes seemed eternal. By the time I ascended to the decompression stops, my head cleared, and, exhilarated, I mentally reconstructed the buzz so I could remember how it felt later.

My most terrifying encounter with narcosis happened while exploring the pitch black pump house of a Japanese war wreck in Palau. After dropping through a hatchway onto the keel, I kneeled down in the four-foot high space and started poking around in the muck for artifacts. My air bubbles hit the fifty-year-old rust just above, causing a thick cloud of orange-brown fog to fall around me. As my vision became obscured, I started to feel terrified, thinking, "I'm trapped at 120 feet, and I'll never find my way out." Narcosis amplified the feeling until I was on the brink of panic. Knowing this was how divers drown with plenty of air left, I thought, "This is stupid. Get a grip. You know how to get out." I had only moved five feet into the compartment, so all I needed to do was stay calm, move directly backward, and feel for the hatchway above. The feeling of relief when I found it did nothing to counteract the pounding adrenaline. I was in clear water again, and my buddy's light was only a few feet away. He was poking around in a wooden box and didn't even realize I was in trouble. After all, I'd only been gone for ten seconds.

Descending on deep sites can be equated to the experience of astronauts on space walks because divers are surrounded by nothing and cling to an umbilical anchor line for direction and security. Even with good visibility one has to follow a sloping descent line for over a hundred feet before the hulking mass of a wreck or bottom appears below.

When I dove on Truk's Aikoku Maru, I anticipated great adventure, but had no idea what I was about to encounter. An American fighter plane's gun camera recorded the sinking of the ship in 1944. The incredible footage showed the ship from above as the plane dove towards it. The image bounced from the recoil of the plane's guns, small explosions erupted all over the deck from hits, and spouting geysers of water surrounded the ship from misses. As the plane's dive got closer, another fighter came into view on a low-level pass. As it cleared the deck, the bomb it dropped landed in a hold full of explosives. The enormous blast that followed disintegrated his plane and severed the ship in half. The Aikoku sank in a few seconds, dragging the crew and 800 infantry soldiers to a watery grave. Only three survived. The ship is now upright in 220 feet of water and looks like it was cut in half with a giant chain saw.

There were five of us diving, including the divemaster who carried a spare tank under his arm with a regulator attached in case any of us needed it. Because of the intense pressure at our deepest point, our air would be consumed six times faster than at the surface. We bunched together on the anchor line and dropped through blue space until the superstructure came into sight. I was buzzed as we passed through 100 feet and knew the narcosis was only going to get more intense.

As we dropped through the galley at 145 feet, I stopped the guide because I couldn't handle the high. The walls closed in on me, and my field of vision narrowed as I fought to stay in control. All I could do was sit still and stare at the wooden decking that hadn't rotted at that depth. After waiting a few minutes, I recovered enough to move around, but knew I couldn't go any deeper.

Aft of the galley, two sets of twin anti-aircraft guns were mounted on the deck — the barrels still pointed skyward. I was delighted when I realized they had been stopped by the blast while firing and must still have live ammunition in the chambers. The guide swam down into a compartment with the others, leaving me alone. A moment later, he returned with something to show me. It was a human skull. He plopped it into my hands. I was still stoned to the bejesus, and my vision again became tunneled. This time I stared into the skull's eye sockets.

PONAPE
Eastern Caroline Islands

"We call it paradise. They call it home." Scott

I landed in Ponape bearing gifts. Dangling from a string in my hand was a ratty cardboard box stuffed to the seams with freshly killed pigeons, presents from friends on Kosrae for their friend Higinio, a man I'd never met who had no idea I was coming. The box didn't look like it was going to last long because of bird fluid saturating the cardboard, so I tried to deliver the gooey thing as fast as I could.

Micronesian back streets aren't named, and proper addresses don't exist, so I ended up tramping out a small odyssey in search of Higinio. By continually asking people, I eventually found someone who gave me his address: over the hill, left at the banana tree, and down next to the mangroves. When I found him, he appreciated the delivery of the oily delicacy by offering to let me sleep on the lanai and use his house as a home base for my travels around the island. When his sister arrived to cook dinner, she was so delighted to find pigeon on the menu, she invited a dozen family members over for chow.

The drug of choice in Ponape is sakau – basically the same stuff as Fijian kava, but the difference is that sakau is concentrated. The syrup that is extracted from the pounding is squeezed through hibiscus fiber to filter out the pulp, ending up with the same consistency as Hawaiian poi. For those who don't know poi, the closest description of it is "gluey," which is why neophytes find themselves straining sakau through their teeth as they drink.

The pounding stones have been around for generations and are shaped like shallow bowls from heavy use. Etched out of porous volcanic rock, they ring when struck. After sunset, villages resonate with the high pitched "bink, bink, bink..." of sakau being pounded outside different huts. When a party gets going, two pounders may use the same stone to meet the larger demand. They pound in an alternating rhythm, creating a "bink-bink, bink-bink, bink-bink..."

Unlike in Fiji, the women of Ponape partake in the festivities. A lot of the older people are hard-core sakau junkies who get snockered nightly. There is no real ceremony involved, but after everyone is sufficiently stoned on the stuff, people start to sing to the rhythm of the pounding. Beautiful harmonies spring up with male and female voices together, an ethereal sound when heightened by the sakau.

Sakau, as far as I can tell, is a tranquilizer (non-alcoholic). One favorite local story is about an Aussie bloke who wandered into a sakau bar, ordered a glass, and fired it down like a shot of booze. (Sipping is not the Australian style). After woofing another round, he ordered a third glass.

The bartender said, "That's not a good idea. This stuff is stronger than you might think."

"Nah, mate, I'm right. Go ahead and give me another."

A few minutes after powering down his third, he got a strange look on his face. Shortly after that, he looked up at the bartender and whimpered, "Help me."

"What's wrong?"

"I can't move."

He was temporarily paralyzed from the neck down, so a couple of Good Samaritans carried him to his hotel and put him to bed. He slept it off, waking up groggy the next day with a newfound respect for pepper root.

After the pigeons were devoured at Higinio's, two of the teenage cousins went to work on the sakau stones. I can't say that I am overly fond of the sakau/kava buzz, but when in Ponape, do as the Pohnpeiians do. Higinio was overjoyed to see me holding my own with the rest of them, but when I got up to take a leak, my legs went off in the wrong direction. The singing stopped momentarily as everyone laughed at the sight of the

56

haole* who was looking at the path to his right while walking into the bushes on his left.

*The other "American" islands in the Pacific have also adopted the word "haole," which is Hawaiian for "foreigner."

ॐ ॐ ॐ

When Higinio was a young boy during World War Two, Japan occupied the central towns on "hub" islands like Ponape. He went to public school, where Japanese was spoken, and remembered the glory days of 1938 to 1943 when he and his schoolmates paraded around the streets in their uniforms yelling, "Banzai!" after victorious battles. When the Americans cut off the Japanese supply lines in 1944, things changed.

The Americans bombed Ponape and bypassed, never invading. There was no way Japan could get supplies to its army, and no way to evacuate them. There were two-and-a-half times more soldiers on the island than Pohnpeiians. When they got hungry, they raided villages, stole food, and forced the people to work for them, causing the locals to flee into the jungle to fend for themselves. The land could not support so many people, a dilemma that was repeating itself on many other Pacific islands at that time. The starving soldiers were eating lizards, insects, geckos, and rats. There are still some isolated islands in Micronesia where Japanese are not welcome because of the harsh way they treated people during the war.

Higinio also hid from the Japanese in the jungle, and cheered in 1944 with other Pohnpeiians as US Navy Corsairs dove down on enemy strongholds, leaving bomb blasts as references for naval bombardment from the new fleet of warships offshore.

ॐ ॐ ॐ

No proper dive shops were operating, so I was directed to a local businessman who, for thirty bucks, provided me with two tanks, weights, an outboard dinghy, and a boat driver.

These were my first coral dives in Micronesia, and I found everything I had hoped for. The reef that ringed the island was shallow in most areas, but in several places, deep-water passages connected the lagoon with the open ocean. I did drift dives through two of these channels by myself with the boat following overhead. Conditions were perfect. I didn't have to swim because the current was strong enough to push me along, and the visibility was 150 feet.

The first dive was Pehleng Passage, a corridor blanketed with corals and stuffed with fish. Right after my descent, a large hawksbill turtle swam past, unconcerned by my presence. Plenty of large silvery tuna, wahoo, and barracuda wandered in from the open ocean. The only proper plants on the reef were ball algae, translucent green spheres the size of golf balls that grew between the corals and sponges. Fan-like bryozoans (branching colonies of individual animals) waved in the surge. Clams had bored themselves into the top of the coral heads, urchins wiggled their spines from niches, and crustaceans hid in crevices underneath. A few moray eels were sticking their heads out of holes with open mouths showing razor sharp fangs. Parts of the reef looked like one of Roger Dean's *Yes* album covers with their bizarre gardens of pillar and elkhorn corals − a perfect place for an hour's solace and meditation.

Staghorn corals poked out of the reef in antler-like branches. Table corals, supported on one "leg" in the middle were flat, thin, and delicate. Brain corals appeared as domed lumps with surface patterns identical to that of a cerebrum. Others also bore resemblance to their namesakes: organ pipe, basket, mushroom, star, tube, and lettuce. They were all sharp enough to have the effect of a cheese grater on me if I was careless, and their stinging cells threatened to add painful insult to injury.

The second dive, Takil Passage, was similar to Pehleng, but had a better invertebrate display. I saw tunicates, christmas-tree worms, nudibranchs, and huge anemones: Tunicates are the link between vertebrates and invertebrates. They have a barrel like body with two openings for nutritive water flow. Primitive spinal columns appear as stunted axial lines in their translucent bodies. Christmas-tree worms live inside calcareous linings in the coral. At the entrance to their hideaways, their heads peek out, adorned with two colorful conical blossoms that spiral upward. If touched, they instantly snap out of sight into the safety of their cocoon-like homes. Nudibranchs look like colorfully patterned slugs, antennae and all, with one exception – there is a flower-like appendage blossoming up from their hindquarters.

The anemones in Takil Passage were up to two feet across. Orange clownfish, immune to their sting, lurked in the tentacles, ready to charge and defend their hosts from any possible attackers. Some of the anemones were closed, possibly digesting fish they had caught. The satiny underside of each of these animals was drawn up to form a lavender ball with tentacle tips protruding through the top. When I waved a thin piece of clamshell near the grasp of one of the open anemones, its tentacles grabbed it and pulled it into its centrally located mouth. A minute later, it realized what it had just eaten and spit it tumbling down the wall to the sand below.

That drew my attention to the base of the reef, where hundreds of cigarette-sized garden eels stuck their serpentine heads up out of their sand holes – resembling a carpet of question marks as they arched into the current, gobbling down passing plankton. As I approached for a better look, they disappeared in unison into the safety of the sand. I backed away, and they rose halfway out. I inched closer, and they ducked down. I waited like a cat over a gopher hole until their heads hesitantly inched back up. Holding my breath so my bubbles wouldn't scare them, I watched the miniature faces of the closest eels as they started picking bites out of the water again.

When I came up, the boat boy pointed to my bare shoulders. I had gotten badly sunburned during the dive. The water was that clear.

Back at the dock, I couldn't pay the boy because I didn't have any cash. Thirty dollars had gone missing from my wallet. Unless a UFO had been beaming up stuff from the boat, the boat boy was the only suspect – not exactly a masterminded crime. I told the kid to give the money to his boss. Apparently, he didn't.

As I was walking back to Higinio's, the irate boss pulled up in his car with the kid in the passenger seat. We ended up at the police station going through an island style legal process. It wasn't the first time the cops had seen the kid, so they started their investigation by searching him. Thirty dollars was found in the cuff of his pant leg. The police chief handed me the money and asked if I wanted to press charges. I said no and thanked him for helping me. The boss was crimson with humiliation. He had taken the problem kid into his home a few years before and had developed more faith in him than the police had. He apologized profusely and refused the thirty dollars for payment, which was fair enough. The worst part was that I had to lug my gear the long way back to Higinio's in the heat.

Ponape is a round volcanic island with lush slopes that angle up from the sea to its center. Rocky plugs and basalt columns poke out of the thick jungle near the summit. The next day, I headed off with the intention of hitchhiking around the island, which worked near the town, but as I got farther out into the boonies, rides became nearly non-existent.

I finally caught one last hop in the back of a Toyota pickup full of other hitchers. Seated with them was Mary, a Peace Corps teacher in her early twenties who was near the end of her two-year stint. When the truck turned off, we hopped out and walked for three hours to her village. We were almost old friends by that point, so she offered me lodging for the night with her host family. I was immersed in another night of wonderful hospitality and sakau harmonies.

In the morning, I packed my bag to set out for the Nan Madol ruins, a two-hour walk away. As I was getting ready to leave, Mary's attention was caught by a radio broadcast in Pohnpeiian. When I started to say goodbye, she held up a finger for me not to talk.

When the announcement was finished, she said, "You might want to wait a day and stick around."

"Why?"

"The king of this half of the island died last night, and the family is going to the funeral. It's a ceremony that only happens a few times every century. You'll see something very unique to this island that few foreigners ever see. Feel free to join us if you'd like."

I set my pack back down.

As she spoke, the islanders were in a mad scramble to find appropriate offerings. Prized hogs were dragged from their pens as young men, still wiping the sleep from their eyes, were ordered to dash into the jungle in search of sakau trees and thousand-pound yams (yes, they can get that big).

Mary explained some of the customs and language we were about to witness:

-There are three Pohnpeiian languages, each used under different circumstances. The seldom spoken royal dialect of Pohnpeiian, not known by lower castes, was to be spoken during the ceremony at the king's home.

-When approaching the king's home, we would do it from the downhill side to show respect.

-Everyone attending the ceremony would bring a generous offering. Our family threw in their best hog along with a yam that turned their pickup truck into a low-rider.

The ceremony started at ten in the morning. New arrivals parked in a field that was a respectful distance from the house. They didn't enter alone, rather, they waited until at least fifty people were present. When they were ready, they would walk up the road in a procession led by three sets of men carrying the new gifts. The first porters in each group hoisted logs across their shoulders with live hogs slung upside down under them. The next set carried monstrous yams lashed on top of wooden frames. The last porters carried unearthed sakau trees, roots and all. Everyone else followed behind.

As each procession arrived, the yams and trees disappeared behind the house, and the pigs were heaped next to a huge bonfire. The men gathered in a large hut, and each, in turn, gave a speech about how great the king was. The women gathered inside the house around the coffin and let out with ear-splitting wails. Then the slaughter of the pigs commenced. One by one, the pigs were stabbed through the ribs with a machete and tossed onto the fire for a few minutes. The expression "screaming like a stuck pig" became a reality for me, and I'll never forget the horrendous stench (nothing like the aroma of a pan full of bacon). The terrified pigs remaining in the pile hyperventilated as they awaited their gruesome end.

After all the pigs were lightly charred, the king's coffin was brought out and lowered into a grave next to his wife's. As it was being filled, six policemen fired a seven-shot salute into the air. (It is common to bury people in the front yard in the Eastern Caroline Islands.)

There were about 500 people in attendance. Mary and I estimated that the hog value was over 50,000 dollars. How many tons of yams and sakau trees could only be wondered at.

This was the first, and biggest, day of a week-long ceremony. As the party broke up, everyone was handed a hunk of pig as they left. The hindquarter I was given I "generously" donated to my hostess. What else was I going to do with a raw pig leg?

ॐ ॐ ॐ

The following day, I was off again on my tour of the island. By late morning, I was marveling at Nan Madol, one of the ancient wonders of the Pacific. The ruins of the ancient city sit out near the barrier reef on mangrove mud flats, well away from the main island. It was constructed, log cabin style, with basalt columns up to forty feet long. The walls are still standing — some at their original height of about twenty feet. Inside are the ruins of palaces, temples, burial places of chiefs, fortresses, turtle pens, and other stone structures. No one knows how this fantastic feat of engineering was carried out; the ancient civilization was long gone before anyone showed up to record it.

After touring the ruins, I caught a ride back to Kolonia in time to join Higinio for a few sunset beers on the lanai. For dinner, Higinio's sister served water buffalo as the entree. It was similar to beef and chewy. When he asked me if I'd like to try dog meat before I left, I thought about the annoying pack of mutts outside that tried to attack me every time I went by and almost said yes, but I wasn't feeling *that* adventurous.

UNSPOILED MICRONESIA
Yap

"Out there where Mike is going, they don't even have dive boats. They paddle out to the dive site on a log, and when they get there the divemaster rolls it real hard, and BAM, they're diving" Mark, my instructor course director, speaking to our class

The three major regions of the Pacific are Micronesia, Polynesia, and Melanesia. Hawaiians are Polynesians, and the people of that region bear a similar resemblance. Micronesians remind me of Central Americans in appearance, and the darker Melanesians look almost African. Micronesia alone covers an area half the size of Africa. Its islands are too numerous to be precisely counted, and most are uninhabited. Many others are relatively untouched by the modern world. A map of the region looks like somebody spilled pepper all over it.

My guidebook said that Yapese women often went bare breasted in public, however, I certainly didn't expect to see that in the international airport. When I walked down the steps from my plane, I was in for a surprise, but not one I had imagined. Most of the old women were topless, but the younger ones were wearing T-shirts. After all, it *was* the twentieth century.

My father has an interesting postwar story about some outlying islands in the vicinity of Yap. On a US Navy destroyer in 1953, he was standing watch when he noticed two raggedy Japanese men paddling a homemade canoe toward the ship. When they got close, the Japanese stood up and waved their arms frantically. They appeared to be stranded soldiers from the war who wanted to get back home, so my dad reported them to the bridge. Anti-Japanese sentiment was still high at that time, and the response from the captain was, "Fuck 'em." The ship sailed on.

The Japanese have all made it home by now, I hope, because some of these islands are boring as hell. Strolling across downtown Yap takes about 45 seconds. There are a couple of restaurants, a filling station, a hardware store, and a one-dock marina in the harbor. For entertainment, you can chew betel nut along with the people who usually loiter on the bench in front of the grocery market. That's as good as it gets. Every now and then, a rickety car adds excitement as it passes. Things hop when an old married couple walks into town. Yapese wives always walk well behind their husbands to show respect, bare breasts bobbing in synch with their lethargic pace. After that, it's back to waiting for the next cloud to pass over the sun, or another bird to fly by. A glob of red betel spit hits the dirt. Time freezes. The scarlet saliva dries slightly as it seeps between the grains of silty sand. Somebody stops to get gas and the crowd goes wild. It's too much to handle at once.

The yards around the village houses are adorned with giant stone coins. This traditional currency consists of monstrous stone discs up to twelve feet in diameter. Some lie flat, others are propped vertically, and a few are even buried. These aragonite monoliths were quarried and hewn in Palau, then towed 800 miles across open ocean on rafts. A hole in the middle allowed land transportation on shouldered logs. Interestingly, the value of a coin is not entirely dependent on size. They are more like pieces of real estate. Every stone has a story, and everyone in its household knows what it is. For example: "That coin in the corner was used by Uncle So-and-so's father to buy old Auntie Ma-as from her family as a wife for him."

Can you imagine what it would be like to have one of these kicking around as chump change? I can.

On a dusty afternoon, the sound of squeaking wagon wheels shatters the normal urban silence of downtown. A crowd of seven forms to see what the commotion is about.

"Lookie there, it's Mike, pullin' his cart into town. He must be comin' to the store to get some vittles and beer, and look, there's a big ol' doubloon about to collapse that little ol' wagon a his."

"Howdy, Mike."

"Howdy. Can anyone spot me some betel nut? I'm fresh out. Hey where's Lester? Oh, hey there, Les. Whaddya say I trade ya this here nugget a limestone for three crates a Spam and every beer that comes on the island between now and Christmas?"

There is actually something to do in Yap besides fantasize about canned goods and symmetric lumps of calcium carbonate, and that is: watch manta rays. A three-day package from the dive shop guarantees manta sightings or your money back. I went out for a day and saw my first mantas at Miil Channel. The bottom of this tidal passageway is shallow, around thirty feet deep. Divers only need to grab a rock and hang on in the current. Sooner or later, the mantas come by. Their grace in the water is accentuated by their size. Several hovered a few feet over me, investigating me the way a horse would with similar walnut eyes.

Mantas love doing loops. Refined elegance best describes a fifteen-foot wide animal smoothly arcing through a thirty-foot circle in less than a second. I developed an immediate fondness for the splendid giants and knew I had to see more . . . and I would, later in Palau.

"If one does not know to which port one is sailing, no wind is favorable." Seneca

If asked about Palau, the average westerner will say, "Never heard of it." I suppose this is why nobody has done much in the way of historical research there. Confronted with an absence of written language and fanciful local legends for sources, historians have understandably given this remote island group, the westernmost in Micronesia, a miss.

I have searched several libraries for information on the area's history, but have only found a half-dozen scholarly references. In general, they stated that Palau was settled by Southeast Asians on a roundabout tour through the Pacific islands 3,000 to 3,500 years ago. Palauans are thought to have a mixed ancestry of Indonesian, Polynesian, and Melanesian based on language, appearance, and, according to the Encyclopedia Britannica, blood type. After the original migration, there is no mention of any further "prehistoric" interaction with Southeast Asia.

My travels through both regions have allowed my amateur observations to blossom into resplendent theories. Mike says Palauans and Asians have been in frequent contact since the original migrations. Let's take a look at proximity, culture and language, and note some evidences.

Published migration maps all look something like this:

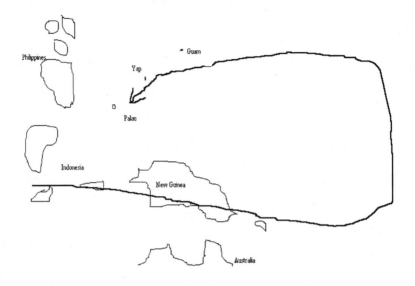

None show any Newtonian shortest distance between two points. Drop the lab notes for a moment and look, professors, and then give the ancient mariners some credit. Mindanao (Philippines) lies only 450 miles from Palau, and Indonesia borders Palau to the southwest.

The traditional sailing canoe of Micronesia is virtually identical to that of the southern Indonesian islands. Its only outrigger is kept to windward while sailing. When tacking, the sail spins around on a center-mounted mast. The bow then becomes the stern as the boat changes direction without turning around.

I once heard Palauans boasting about one of their clever traditional fishing techniques. Apparently, they trolled for fish by trailing their lines under kites. In Lombok, Indonesia, a thousand miles away, I was amazed to see local fishermen stand on the reef with kites flying from their fishing poles. When a fish got hooked underneath, the kite fell, and the two were reeled in together.

In the Philippines, Thailand, and Indonesia, I saw people from seafaring coastal villages who could easily pass for Palauans (seafaring, as in, sailing around a lot). The look-alikes have the Palauan features of darker skin, kinky hair as opposed to straight, and flatter noses with noticeable bridges. Compared with other Micronesians, Palauans generally have flatter, more Asian facial features.

Melodies of Palauan songs seemed to be virtually repeated in the Philippines and Indonesia. I couldn't tell the difference between live nightclub bands in any of those countries when they sang traditional songs.

The most notable example of Palauan artistry is in the painted decorations of the village bais (traditional meetinghouses). One popular design is that of a woman, sitting in full frontal nudity with her legs wide open. This very inviting pose is identical to images found in the cave art of Kakadu National Park in northern Australia (yet another land in relatively close proximity). Palauan bais are also similar to Indonesian longhouses in appearance. (Another similarity in the region: the religious monoliths on the island of Sumba (Indonesia) have an uncanny resemblance to the massive "latte" stones of Guam in both size and shape.)

Some words in the Malay dialects are identical to Palauan, such as "kau" (you). Others are very similar, such as the word for no. In Indonesia it is "tidak" (pronounced tee-dahk). In Palau, it is "ngdiak," which sounds more like "dee-ahk" when spoken. In the Philippines, "Yes," in Tagalog is "oh oh." In Palauan, it is "oh oi." I had heard that Palau got its name from a Spanish or Portuguese word (palo) that obscurely refers to a type of tree. I had real doubts about that after learning that the word for island in Malay is "pulau."

71

For these peoples to be in contact so long ago, they must have been incredible mariners who sailed canoes between small islands in the vast open ocean. This is interesting from our western standpoint because as far as I know, it was seldom or never discussed in our public schools. All Americans know about Leif Ericson, the Viking sailor, but I'd have to say the Micronesians have him beat. Navigating to a tiny island in a vast expanse of sea is a fair bit harder than bumping into the coast of North America.

Without written directions, one trick to ancient Micronesian navigation was to carefully watch the wave and wind patterns while sailing and put the resulting route into song lyrics. The navigators then sang their way across the Pacific the way aboriginal Australians sang their way across Australia. For example, an aboriginal verse might have gone something like this: "Turn right at the big red rock at the end of the day to find the water hole." A Micronesian verse could have been, "Stay to the left of the red star when it's setting."

It's an old trick for students to put words to music for rote memorization because songs stick in the memory better. When I was a kid, there was an educational TV commercial that taught us the Preamble to the Constitution with a sing-along (Schoolhouse Rock). I can easily sing that insipid tune today with all the words, but don't ask me about Latin names for fossils that I *didn't* sing in college. (From a Darwinian perspective, this may help explain the popularity of music among us higher primates.)

On an interesting side note, many Micronesian words and family names are western, an indication of how explorers, traders, colonists, and missionaries have wandered through these islands over time. The first Europeans to influence the islands were from Spain. In Palau, the word for watermelon is Spanish — "sandia." Spain ruled Guam for over 230 years before becoming a US territory. Many Chamorros, the native inhabitants of Guam and the other Marianas Islands, have Spanish surnames. Germany settled Micronesia from 1899 until 1914. On Ponape, my friend Higinio's last name was Germanic. On Truk, someone told me that dogs are referred to as "kmeers" from "Komm her" (come here). Glass windows were introduced to the region in the late nineteenth century, and the Palauan word for window is the same in German (Fenster). Palauan rubber bands (kummi) must have appeared during this time, also, because "Gummi" means "rubber" auf Deutsch. The most prevalent pre-American influence on the languages is Japanese. They had control of the islands from 1914 to 1945. "Kampai" is the most common drink toast now. With the exception of Guam and the rest of the Marianas Islands, more Japanese surnames exist than any others. Japanese is still spoken as a second language by many old people, of whom many have a Japanese grandparent or two, and chopsticks are still served in Micronesian table settings along with knives, forks, and spoons.

GOOD TIMING
Palau

"The only problem with this paradise is that once your beer gets warm, it's gonna stay that way." Tommy

It was in the stars. I heard from divers in Truk that an American guy in Palau named Sam was looking for a divemaster. I mailed my resume to him, letting him know that I would be arriving two weeks afterward.

On my first day in Palau, I explored Koror, where several villages had grown together to form the main town. I enjoyed the ripe-orange fragrance of the frangipani trees that lined the streets as I wandered past restaurants, a small college, a few nightclubs, some stores, and a gas station. Administration buildings took up most of the center because, as I later found out, more than fifty percent of the workforce is on the government payroll.

Near the causeway, a scraggly-bearded white man wearing only a pair of ripped up denim shorts walked barefoot out of a store with two six-packs of Bud under his arm.

When he saw me, he said, "Hey, you're new in town. Want to go check out some rock islands?"

"Sure."

"Come on, then."

His boat was tied up across the street. Coincidentally, I had just met Scott, Sam's other divemaster.

After weaving through beautiful waterways for twenty minutes, we scrambled through a hole in the side of one of the 700 rock islands of Palau — steep-sided masses of limestone, varying in size from one-bush islets to rain-forested expanses. This one opened up into a fifty-foot wide circular grotto, surrounded on all sides by overhanging cliffs. Vines dangled down from the forest above.

That's where Scott filled me in on Sam. Twenty-odd years before, the future high chief of Palau was stationed at Fort Lewis, Washington, where he met and married Sam's mother. When he was appointed to be the traditional leader of Palau, the Army granted him a discharge, and he returned to his native land. After Sam graduated from high school, he came out to visit and stayed, eventually marrying a Palauan woman. His first job was working in a restaurant kitchen for a typical Palauan wage — a dollar an hour. Sam was more enterprising than that, so with a few tanks and a hand-me-down boat from the chief, he started his dive operation. His "dive shop" wasn't much; the boat was kept at a public dock, the equipment room was the back of his house, a small compressor was stashed inside the government warehouse, and his pickup truck was used to run in between. Scott also explained that Sam had another divemaster who was leaving within a week, and that my timing was perfect. I had a beer with Sam that afternoon (six hours after my plane had landed) and started working the next day. With less than a hundred dives under my belt, I had gotten hired in the world's greatest dive locale, best known for drift diving along bottomless walls in fast currents full of big fish and sharks.

Sam had squatted an abandoned boat, the *Hose Queen*, and agreed to let me live on it. I towed it into a hidden inlet less than a mile from town. Although civilization was close, the only sights and sounds in my new home were natural. Surrounded by jungled limestone cliffs, my hideaway was the ultimate sanctuary. Parrots, fruit bats, and cockatoos flew in and out of the trees, and juvenile fish lived in the calm waters until they were big enough to move out to the barrier reef. Turtles, sea snakes, moray eels, and crocodiles occasionally wandered by. Rainbows appeared in the cove against the backdrop of green jungle while corals glimmered through the calm surface of the water. Every morning at dawn, I awoke to the splashing of blue-finned trevally feeding on schools of smaller fish around the boat. Their powerful tails ripped the surface as the terrified schools jumped in bounding arcs. Squawking long-tailed birds got in on the action, catching these airborne snacks or plucking them from the surface.

It wasn't long before I had a local girlfriend, Christine, to spend nights with me. Lying on a blanket on the deck, we sometimes stayed up until the dawn hours, staring out through the shadow of the earth and marveling at the heavens' progress as our little planet rotated. I had found the ultimate home and lifestyle – true paradise.

BAD PROFILES
Palau

"Ignorance is bliss." Scott

Dive tables are used to determine safe maximum dive times to avoid decompression sickness (the bends). A dive profile is the architecture of a dive — a time versus depth graph of a diver's position that is often drawn during pre-dive briefings. Ideally, it should be U-shaped, showing a descent to the deepest point followed by a gradual ascent to shallow water before surfacing. The slow ascent allows nitrogen to dwindle out of the body during the dive, reducing the chance of decompression sickness. However, many beginners become distracted under water and bounce around from discovery to discovery, creating a "sawtooth" profile.

Dive computers, small enough to be worn on a wrist, calculate nitrogen uptake under water and display safe allowable bottom times to the diver throughout the dive. Unfortunately their use can lead to a false sense of security, unable to warn against unsafe techniques like following bad profiles.

During my first stint in Palau, I was briefly haunted by a spell of dangerous diving stunts, wacky divers, and underwater ghosts. For three days, the overlying lattice of coincidence did nothing but dump all its sideshow freaks on me. On Monday morning this cast of characters consisted of two pilots from different airlines, a South African woman, an American dive instructor on vacation, and the Odd Family, whose behavior was displaced from a 1950's sitcom — far too blessed with joy to be real.

79

Waiting on board for the curtain to go up, the supporting characters fussed with their equipment while the Odd Family warmed up for the first act. Mother chatted happily about the achievements of their two fine sons while they nodded along on cue. Father stood behind them, patting their shoulders approvingly.

Father had an enormous beak of a nose and the hint of a mustache. Mother had a little dumpling nose. The boys had a hereditary blend of both. I can't describe them any better even though I spent days with them because their eyes were hidden behind sunglasses, their faces were caked in white sun block, and the rest of them was sealed up in head-to-toe Lycra bunny suits that Mother had sewn for them because Father was a physician paranoid about skin cancer. The neon outfits each had a distinctive geometric pattern. Dad's was snot-green triangles on a red background. Mom was in navy-blue dots on orange. The fourteen-year old sported pink tiger-stripes on blue, and the sixteen-year old was broadcasting orange and white squares over black. How any self-respecting teenagers could let their parents make them wear those suits was beyond me. Under water, they stole the show. The exhaust air from their regulators filled up their bunny hoods, causing the material to float to a point above their heads. When the psychedelic coneheads followed me around the dive sites, the fish stopped to stare at *us*.

The South African closed the day's performance when she thrust her dive computer in front of me after the last dive and asked if I could get it to work. The console displayed a one-minute stop at ten feet. The reason it wasn't working was because it was locked out, indicating that she couldn't safely surface yet. She had run it into decompression and missed the stop. In lieu of dive tables and reading the directions for her computer, she had used stupidity to guide her through the dive. I told her to watch for signs of decompression sickness for the next twenty-four hours and not to dive with us again.

Tuesday — Act Two

In the morning, word got back to me that my leading actors were causing a stir in the community in their free time. From the moment they paraded out of their hotel wearing their resplendent attire, they turned heads. In a small town like Koror, they became instant celebrities. It was hard enough for *me* to fathom, but the *islanders* were aghast. The Odds went everywhere in their brilliant suits, waving to onlookers, scaring land crabs back into their holes, and tempting boat crews to jump overboard.

That afternoon featured the airline pilots' dual performance on their final day of diving. The second dive was planned for sixty feet, but one of them went down to a hundred without a computer. I chased after him and motioned for him to ascend. He shook his head no. I kept after him until he relented, but he was furious after I had him finish the rest of the dive in shallow water. After listening to his angry complaints, I countered with a stern lecture on how bent divers can become paralyzed or killed. I wondered how a professional pilot trained for technical perfection, awareness of pressure changes, and redundant safety measures could be so haphazard with his personal safety.

The other pilot was alone in Palau on a layover so I invited him to dinner. After dumping our gear off, we took the boat over to the dock of my favorite restaurant and had a good meal to finish off an awesome day in the water. While paying the bill at the cash register, I felt pressure against my back and realized that he was leaning gently against me. Wondering why he was being so friendly, I turned and watched him fall away like a tree headed for the sawmill. He hit the floor hard and then jumped quickly back to his feet.

Embarrassed, he said, "Sorry, I fell asleep for a second."

"Fell asleep?"

"Yeah, I do that sometimes."

I envisioned a scene in a 727 as he made an announcement over the intercom: "Sorry about that 10,000 foot nose-dive, folks. I took a quick nap."

The first scene featured a cameo by a Japanese guest star — this was strange because Japanese tourists in Palau dive exclusively with Japanese dive companies.

After lunch, as everybody was gearing up for the second dive, I noticed him relaxing and asked, "Are you going to do the next dive?"

"No. I don't think so. I want to take it easy today because I drowned yesterday."

"You . . . WHAT?"

"I drowned yesterday. The last thing I remember, I was at ninety feet. The crew said they found me on the surface and brought me back to life with CPR."

"Are you kidding me?"

"No, the only reason I'm diving with you guys is because nobody else would take me out today."

"Thanks *a lot,* buddy."

We left him on the boat under the watchful eye of Scott, the captain, and jumped in at Blue Corner for the second dive. While hanging onto the lip of the reef at sixty feet with everyone watching the fish action, I entered The Twilight Zone. The Odds huddled in dazzling formation to my left while the American instructor stayed to my right. His equipment, unlike their neon, was all black: mask, wetsuit, fins, the works — an uncommon combination. His medium-length gray hair offered the only contrast to his commando-like appearance. Equipped with a Nikonos camera and a computer, he indicated that he wanted to go by himself to a deeper depth and let the current carry him around the point. I knew he was an expert diver so I shrugged "okay." He gave me a thankful nod and disappeared over the edge. Ten minutes later, he swam up from behind and resumed his position next to me on the edge of the reef.

After another ten minutes, the Odds were low on air, so I sent them up together. After a running bottom time of forty-five minutes, I looked at my computer. I had five minutes left at that depth. Since the instructor had gone over the wall, his remaining time would be less. I reached over to check his computer. It wasn't there. He had a Nikonos camera, black mask, black fins, black wetsuit, black fins, and gray hair, but it wasn't the same guy. I'd never seen this diver before. Where did he come from? Where was his dive group? Where was his *divemaster*?

I left him and ascended. The Odds and the American instructor were not only on the boat, they were already dry, a situation that made me look highly unprofessional.

Scott said, "Well, well, well. If it isn't the Lone Ranger."

"You're not going to believe this, but . . . "

THE BAD CANADIAN
Palau

"Nobody hates a Canadian." Kathy

If there is one thing worse than bad divers, it's FAT bad divers, because the extra lead required to sink them causes horrid extremes in otherwise manageable buoyancy problems. The objective is neutral buoyancy, neither sinking nor floating. If these divers happen to be clumsy as well, this is as easy as getting the Hindenburg to fly, or the Titanic to float. When I refer to FAT, by the way, I don't mean people who suck in around mirrors, rather those who slow down or squeeze through doorways. The Bad Canadian squeezed.

She worked in the embassy in Manila, and as far as I can guess, grumbled all day under fluorescent lighting while playing with rubber stamps that read REJECTED or EVICTED. On the boat, she sat silently to the side, snarling at the rest of us while we had a good time without her. Under water, she stared catatonically at rocks instead of fish. As tour leader, I felt I should bring her around to join us in our merriment, but she rejected all invitations. After trying fruitlessly, I felt like giving the vile beast a TV remote control and sending her back to the couch in her living room.

To top things off, she insisted on wearing a thick (seven millimeter) wetsuit top despite the 86 degree water. Thick wetsuits require considerable extra lead on the weight belt. The Bad Canadian's belt weighed in at a whopping twenty-nine pounds (twenty more than the average). I knew her blubber would keep her warm enough, so I tried to dissuade her from wearing the suit. However, she clung to that lump of rubber like a teddy bear, defiantly ignoring my advice like she ignored my dive briefings.

As increasing water pressure crushes its air spaces, a neoprene foam wetsuit loses flotation. Divers need to add air to their inflatable BC (buoyancy compensator) vests to offset this. Conversely, divers must release air from their BCs on ascent. Expansion and compression of any air in the BC exacerbates the problem. Failure to make proper adjustments results in a runaway ascent (Polaris missile), or a runaway descent (Look out below!). It took the miscreant days to realize this so I spent entire dives lugging her around by the tank valve. She was too big to be doing pachinko ball imitations on the reef.

By her fifth day, she seemed able to dive alone, so I turned my attention elsewhere. The afternoon dive was Turtle Cove, a vertical wall with no bottom in sight. Descending with the divers through a hole in the reef, I glimpsed a falling object out of the corner of my eye. The Bad Canadian was immobile, staring straight ahead, and accelerating rapidly toward the depths. There was a narrow ledge seventy feet below, and she hit it, blasting a cloud of sand up that obscured her from sight. I went down, and despite all temptation, did not roll her over the edge. Instead, I added air to her BC and towed her along again. A remnant of her crater still shows on that ledge, and it has become a regular part of my Turtle Cove dive briefing.

FISH DAYDREAMS
Palau

"Sometimes it's a hard world for small things." H.I.

When asked where my favorite dive site is, I never hesitate to say New Dropoff. This underwater peninsula juts out like a thumb from Palau's barrier reef into the Philippine Sea. Living organisms are rooted into every square inch of it, covering the hard coral ridge with a soft colorful mantle. The exquisite natural architecture is fascinating, but the real entertainment is provided by the fish. When the tides change, strong currents wash fresh nourishment over the point, attracting tiny plankton feeders. These smaller fish draw larger predators that in turn attract the sharks. It doesn't take long for every link in the food chain to appear.

On the tip of the point, two wide vertical grooves add personality to the reef. The larger of these cuts drops to 120 feet, where a fantastic collection of wire corals and fans stick out from the wall. Sailfish, thresher sharks, oceanic whitetip sharks, and massive tuna cruise this neighborhood. Farther down, at the base of the smaller cut, the reef begins to overhang. At the base of this prominence is a small cave with an arch at its entrance. From there, the point looms above like the prow of a magnificent living ship, cutting the transparent water on an endless voyage. Below, a steep sandy incline drops 12,000 feet to the ocean floor.

When the current is strong, the vertical corridor of the smaller cut becomes a giant fire hose, funneling water straight up from the depths. A school of snapper loves to hover in the heart of the shaft when the torrent is rushing, and whenever a fresh gust barrels through, the hardy fish are tossed around like autumn leaves on a sidewalk. The blast continues fifty feet past the edge of the reef to the surface, where it "boils" hard enough to flatten waves — a helpful "landmark" when looking for the dive site.

Above the cuts, the reef flattens and stretches for hundreds of yards. Turtles wander this area, whitetip reef sharks lie in sand holes, and octopus slither from crevice to crevice. Alert divers occasionally notice manta rays passing overhead.

When the current kicks up over two knots at the tops of the cuts, the fish pack together to form a living fog-layer. A diver's objective is to get into that haze, hang on to the reef to maintain position, and spend the dive in sensory overload. Small fish dart back and forth among the coral heads, selecting their planktonic provisions. Schools of larger fish hover nearby in clouds. The largest fish hang out in twos or threes like schoolyard bullies, ready to dash in and gobble up any inattentive little guys. Dozens of gray reef sharks cruise past, arrogantly eyeing the buffet.

The most prominent predators are trevally, two-foot-long streamlined ocean swimmers whose silvery hides are tipped with yellow and blue fins. When a languid trevally spies a school of savory hors d'oeuvres and decides to *do lunch*, it snaps its tail hard, instantly accelerating into a carnivorous blur. I thought life on land was mean until I saw what goes on under water. Fish can't take coffee breaks. If they drop their guard for a second, they're snacks. Too bad Darwin wasn't a diver. He would have loved it.

When the current rips hard enough to suck divers' bubbles over the other side of the reef and down out of sight, the smaller fish swim hard or hide in the coral to keep from getting washed away. Only the hydrodynamic sharks soar effortlessly, similar to hawks on a windy day. They often glide up a few feet over the lip and hang in place. Once, in a moderate current, I carefully watched a shark doing this, and noticed that its angle of attack into the current was slightly downward. It was falling through the water, but motionless relative to the reef. I got an idea and tried it out. I exhaled hard and held my breath out to sink. I then straightened my body and angled downward. It worked! I could let go of the reef, breathe shallowly, and maintain my position with a minimal amount of fin twitching. By sloping my right shoulder down, I was able to glide slowly towards the shark until we were side-by-side, three feet apart. A few minutes later, another shark appeared, coming straight at me. When his mouth was two feet from my face, I realized that my head could easily fit inside it. I lost my nerve, gave up my spot, and swam over to join the other divers in relative safety.

This reef is also a great place to watch cleaning wrasse at work. These finger-sized colorfully striped fish run the cleaning stations in their neighborhoods. A cleaning station is the car wash of the reef. Larger fish pull up to the station, sometimes lining up behind each other to let the wrasse work over their skin, mouth, and teeth for parasites. They lift their heads and open their mouths, gills, and fins to let the smaller fish go to work. When they are finished, they wander off so the wrasse may attend to the next fish.

Surgeonfish add to the show by slowly changing the color of their bodies. Over the space of a minute, dark brown hides will flash three silver stripes across their skin, then fade to silvery light blue before returning to dark brown. Other surgeon species will go from dark brown with darker brown spots to brilliant blue with yellow gold near the head. Even their eyes change color!

When a shark pulls up, it doesn't wait in line. The others back off as the big fish holds open a yawn, allowing the wrasse to swim through its gill slits, clean its teeth from the inside, and exit through its mouth. Eating a cleaning wrasse is strictly taboo. In this symbiotic relationship, one gets fed, and the other gets cleaned. It is perfection in nature . . . almost − I once watched a large gray snapper seemingly daydream while it was being cleaned. It forgot there was a wrasse in its mouth and shut it. It seemed to gag a little, but nothing else happened. Several minutes later, I still hadn't seen the wrasse emerge.

I yelled through my regulator, "You're not supposed to do that!"

ENTANGLED
Palau

"Don't stress. When you stress, you can't function." Bjorn

Just because Scott and I were each taking out groups of twelve Taiwan Chinese divers (far from the world's best) during the day and pulling it off, we assumed we could do it at night. We gave each of them a green glow stick to attach to their tank valves, and, being oh-so-smart, took an orange one for ourselves so they'd know whom to follow.

We anchored at sunset near a Japanese war wreck in the harbor channel and waited for darkness. We started the dive in a moderate current and drifted down the reef to sixty feet. From there, I led them through inky black water towards the wreck. After a minute, its steel hulk loomed up, brilliantly adorned by colorful coral polyps. Things were going smoothly until I rounded the stern and got carried away in the current. When I checked the group, only ten lights were behind me, so I started swimming back to wait for the last two. I wasn't making any headway, but I could hold my position relative to the wreck. Night dives are disorienting enough without unforeseen course reversals. This change in direction confused everyone, so what did they do? They went to the orange glow stick on my tank, and crammed in together as if they were on a Taipei bus at rush hour. By the time the last two divers came around the stern, I was packed tightly in a neoprene mass of bodies. I couldn't kick my legs to swim or even shove people with my arms. A vision of impending death went through my head.

Every which way I turned, they smacked onto me like bugs being drawn to a light bulb. What could I do? I got an idea, turned off my light, hid my glow stick in my hand, and exhaled hard. My negative buoyancy sank me into the darkness below,

91

and I was free. I swam out in front of them before turning my light back on. As soon as they saw the orange glow stick in front of them, they charged after me again. Fins don't fail me now. I fled for the boat to elude a grisly fate.

BOTTOM TIME
Palau

"The first sign of a nervous breakdown is when you start thinking your work is terribly important." Milo

One of the most popular Palauan dives is Chandelier Cave, a pear shaped cavern with an entry hole at thirty feet. Inside, four main air chambers can be reached on scuba. When divers come up, they can remove their regulators and float around in their inflated BC jackets. The first air pocket is the most beautiful. Columnar walls divide the space into explorable passageways. The second, an elongate chamber, features a flowstone curtain along one wall. The last two rooms each connect into a basketball-court-sized room above sea level. Scuba gear can be left floating as divers clamber up through muddy holes to get inside. Part of my standard upper room tour was having the group shut off their flashlights to experience absolute darkness.

I was attracted immediately to Monica when she started diving with us. I had no idea at the time that I would later visit her at her home in Bermuda and end up living with her there.

I didn't make any passes at her during the first few days. I only bit my lip and ogled as she suntanned on the deck, her brown skin darkening to satiny double espresso. At the end of the third day, she asked if she could dive the famous cave. In chamber three, we left our gear, dropped our fins on a ledge, and clambered up into the upper cave. During the lights out part of the tour, I felt something brush my cheek. She was looking for my lips . . . with her own. Within minutes, wetsuits were unzipped and bikini strings unknotted. If I had anticipated it, I could have brought candles, music, and wine. Instead we had an unaccompanied tumble by flashlight, furrowing the soft mud on the floor of the cave.

Dive time — 72 minutes.

Air used — 300 psi.

Just trying to keep the customers satisfied.

BERMUDA AND THE CARIBBEAN

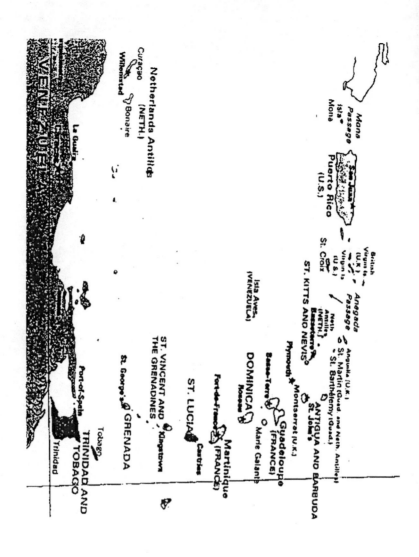

NIGHT DIVING
Saint Thomas, US Virgin Islands

"I've experienced nighttime at dozens of tropical resort islands, and they all have one thing in common. Divemasters and instructors drink a lot." Scott

The sharks of Saint Thomas were the most aggressive I've seen. Their behavior was a result of the island's male to female ratio, which was roughly ten to one. Whenever an unaccompanied woman walked into a bar, conversation stopped as fins sprouted out of men's backs. Within seconds, one would be next to her, trying his best lines, while the bartender lined the tabletop with cocktails sent by hopeful horn-dogs in the bleachers.

Frenzies abounded at ladies' night in all of the local taverns. After work, single men threw on their best T-shirts and converged devoutly on the night's hot spot. Their mission: get hammered during happy hour before drink prices went up.

The place was overrun with dive instructors, but most of them had given it up for jobs that paid better, like waiting tables. Like everyone else, they had come from the States to find their Eden. My roommate was a typical example: recently divorced, burnt out on working conditions in the real world, mid-thirties, and wanting to get his youthful *ya-yas* out while he could. He became a dive instructor for no other reason than to be able to find a job at his tropical escape. He taught scuba for eight hours a day and chased women for ten. After work, he'd change into his volleyball outfit and head for the beach. He rarely played because he was busy hitting on every woman between fifteen and fifty. Every morning on my way to work, I'd survey the shoes by the door to figure out who was in his bed — someone new, or someone I'd already met.

Our favorite hangout was Poor Man's Bar, where we had the opportunity to roll dice with the bartender to decide who paid for the drink. If we won, the drink was on the house. If we lost, we paid double which was still a great deal because we mixed our own drinks. That's right. For two bucks, the bartender served a sixteen-ounce plastic cup full of ice and lined up whatever bottles we requested on the bar top. A swizzle stick was provided, but straws and umbrellas weren't. Poor Man's was seldom visited by ladies or gentlemen.

Our buddy Tony was a hilarious little drunk. One night, in a condition somewhere between invisible and bulletproof, he walked into Poor Man's and ordered an Absolut Cranberry. He rolled for it and cheered when double sixes came up. As he jubilantly filled his cup to the brim with vodka and added a dash of cranberry juice, the barkeep put a death gaze on him. It wasn't polite to applaud if you won.

Tony noticed the glare and confessed, "I had to win because I didn't have any money left."

The bartender, whose ancestry appeared to be neo-primordial, lowered his eyebrows and glowered harder.

Tony regained an inkling of composure and realized his mistake. "What would have happened if I had lost?"

The cromag pointed at the exit.

We loaned Tony four bucks so he wouldn't have any further clashes with the lesser primate, but as soon as he got the cash, he made things worse by waving it over the bar.

After deciding to head home, we were waiting outside for Tony. Suddenly, his body came flying out of the entrance above us. After somersaulting and bouncing down two flights of stairs, he landed with a resounding thud on the pavement at our feet. Then he jumped up and joined us as though nothing out of the ordinary had happened.

"Are you okay?"

"Yeah."

"Didn't that hurt."

"Well, yeah, it hurt a little."

"A little?"

"Well, a lot, actually."

"What happened?"

"Whaddya think happened? That bartender threw me out because I wanted a road beer and lost the roll."

১ ১ ১

New divers often join the ranks of the local lushes after the last day of instruction. Once, my students, all male, celebrated by hauling me down to Frenchtown, a quaint restaurant district of Charlotte Amalie. After way too many kamikazes, one grabbed a piece of cold spaghetti from the plate and snorted one end of it up his nose until it was almost gone. While holding the end that was dangling from his nostril, he coughed up the original end through his mouth and grabbed it with his fingers. Then he started drawing the spaghetti strand back and forth, flossing his sinuses. This was the grossest thing I'd seen since my college roommate lit his own farts, but with a skinful of Absolut, it was pretty funny. Unfortunately, the waiter didn't see it that way and threatened to eighty-six all of us unless the spaghetti snorter promised to cease and desist. I told my student he'd make a great divemaster someday.

BOTTLED UP
Saint Thomas, USVI

"Without beer, life as we know it could not exist." Mosier

"Hey, Matt. You wanna go for a dive?" I asked from my boat in the adjacent slip.

Matt took a moment to respond. "I'd be up for a bottle dive."

His bare feet were on the instrument panel of the parasail boat. His butt was firmly planted where it belonged – in the captain's chair. A joint was lodged between his first and middle fingers.

"What's a bottle dive?"

"You go look for old bottles."

"What's so great about that?"

"It's intense." Matt's words strained out in a tiny cloud of smoke as he held his breath in.

"I'll give it a shot. When do you want to do it?"

Matt shot a glance at the afternoon sun, calculating how much optimum dive time was left in the day. "Now."

"Let's go."

We pulled out two full tanks and loaded our dive bags into Matt's boat. With the roach between his lips, he roared the monstrous engine to life. Vibration pounded through the air as I cast off the lines.

Matt idled over to the *Bo Hawg*. "Hey Rocky, want to drive for us while we do a dive?"

Rocky appeared from below, rum and coke in hand. "Sure. Where ya goin?"

"Just over to the cay."

"Hang on a sec while I button up." Rocky disappeared below.

Matt eased the speedboat up against the *Piglet*, Rocky's dinghy.

Rocky appeared topside again with his fingers wrapped around the necks of three Heinekens. He locked the hatchway before sea-legging it across the dinghy's bench to us.

"They're not getting any colder."

"Greenies" in hand, we stood next to Matt as he nosed the boat out of the marina.

When we were clear of the stone breakwater, Matt said, "Hang on," and dumped the throttle forward. If he hadn't warned us, we would have tumbled ass over heels into the transom.

"Whoa! That's some acceleration you got there. I couldn't have stuck my tongue out if I'd tried." Rocky hadn't been on the boat when it was empty of customers before.

Matt smiled and said, "Hang on" again, and pushed the throttle all the way down.

Desperately trying to keep the beer in our bottles, we let out a whoop. At sixty knots, life is beautiful.

The cay wasn't far, so I readied the anchor as Matt approached the east end of the tiny island. When he slowed and gave me a nod, I flung it into fifty feet of water.

Matt shut down the beast below and went straight into a dive briefing. "This is my secret spot, so don't tell anyone where it is. There used to be a whorehouse over on that beach back in the 1800's, and this was the anchorage. Every time the tide changes, the sand moves and uncovers virgin bottles. Don't pick up anything that has a lip for a metal cap or screw threads. That stuff is too new. Look for rounded or cone shaped mouths. Don't bother with anything broken, either. If you have any doubts, ask me. I'll give thumbs up for a keeper or thumbs down for junk. The current is running hard, so go for anything you can as fast as you can. Max depth is eighty. Stay for thirty minutes. Rocky, stick with our bubbles pretty close, okay?"

"Got it."

As soon as we hit the water, Matt swam hard to eighty feet. I tore after him and moved off to the side so we wouldn't search the same area. He was right about the current. As we were washed over the sandy bottom, we barely had time to dash back and forth between glass protuberances. At first, every bottle I pulled was a dud. Some were liquor. Others were beer. One was Aunt Jemima syrup. A few I didn't recognize. I showed them only to get a disdainful thumbs down.

After twenty-six minutes, I snatched at a green square and yanked it out. Embossed in the glass was "J. H. HENKE S." I held it up. Matt smiled behind his mouthpiece and gave me a thumbs up. That was my beginner's luck dive.

That night, Matt showed off his collection. His favorites were handmade torpedo bottles, football-shaped flasks with intentionally rounded bottoms that required them to lie flat so their corks wouldn't dry out. Others were spun in wooden molds while being blown, clearly showing trapped air bubbles. Some were short and squat. All held corks at one time. We figured my bottle was for bitters or gin and over a hundred years old.

&? &? &?

Three months later, I was in bottle diver's heaven — Bermuda. Crazed with my newest hobby, I plundered underwater debris fields until my BC could barely lift my collecting bag.

One afternoon, I came across a strange round-bottomed flask, freshly uncovered and free from growth. The rubber washer was still intact in the neck. Raised lettering said, "Gosling Bros Hamilton & St Georges Bermuda," and around the base in small type, "Wm Barnard & Sons London." Inside the crimped neck was a marble. I didn't know what it was, but when I brought it aboard, the captain went crazy with envy. I had found a true prize. Marble seltzer bottles were popular at the beginning of the twentieth century, but are extremely rare because children often broke them to get the glass ball out. Held against the mouth of the flask by the pressure of the soda, the marble was pushed down to open the bottle. The bottles had two inside grooves to trap the glass ball away from the opening when pouring.

My collection today is puny compared to Matt's, but it's a start. I've got several wood-cast bottles, but no torpedoes yet.

WHALE WATCHING
Bermuda

"What do fat people have a lot of?" Kyle's axiom

Bermuda is one of the wealthiest islands in the world, boasting, among other things, an official unemployment rate of zero for its 62,000 people. This crescent-shaped former British territory stretches for twenty-two miles along the southern edge of a volcanic seamount, roughly a thousand miles east of South Carolina. The Gulf Stream warms the waters enough for tropical marine life to flourish, and Caribbean-like beaches line the southern side of the island.

Bermuda is famous for its golf courses, onions, and brightly-colored knee-length shorts that businessmen wear with conservative dress shirts, jackets, and ties. The police also preserve this tradition, a big hit for camera wielding tourists. The white-roofed houses that dot the hillsides are painted in traditional pastel colors that mirror the businessmen's shorts. Tourism is a multimillion dollar a year economy on this neat and tidy island. Even the Swiss are surprised by its cleanliness. Ordinances prohibit billboards, large signs, litter, or any other unsightly items that might discourage visitors.

The coral reefs aren't big walls, but they are riddled with arches, caves, and hundreds of alluring, explorable tunnels. The most famous is the Cathedral Room, a fifty-foot-high underwater chamber with several small holes in the ceiling just below the surface. Flickering columns of sunlight stream into the dark cavern through these holes, creating a bouncing laser effect.

Ships have been hitting the shoals around the island since the Atlantic was first navigated, creating an undersea maritime history museum. There isn't much left of the old wooden ships except cannons, but some of the newer ones are still in fair shape. One of the best is an upright Civil War steamer with intact paddle wheels.

Because of Bermuda's other tourist attractions and proximity to the US, most of the divers that flood in are novices who require a fair amount of assistance from divemasters. One particular type needs even more help — those in the heavyweight division. These customers not only rock the boat; they threaten to sink it. The undisputed world title in this weight class belonged to the Fat Family: husband Bill, wife Marcia, and daughter Tanya — all freshly graduated from their basic dive course.

Before we hit the water, Bill confided in me that he was delighted that he had found a family activity that they could all enjoy. Skiing hadn't worked because Marcia was unable to get out of a lift chair. As it turned out, she couldn't get out of the water, either.

To get Marcia back on the boat, I would first get all of the equipment and Tanya aboard. Then Marcia would get her feet on the lowest ladder rung while Tanya and I pulled like crazy on her arms. Bill, in the water, would grab the ladder and drive his shoulder up into her butt. The bow lifted as everyone's weight almost sunk the stern, but after a lot of grunting and thrashing around, we always managed to land her.

At least the Fat Family was nice. With some of the other heavyweights, I wasn't so fortunate.

One morning, a tubby customer walked up holding a mouthpiece. "Hey, put this on for me. It's custom made and I don't want one of those crappy ones that everybody's been slobbering all over."

"Sure."

He pushed it into my hand. "And give me eight pounds on my weightbelt, too."

I've never worked in a circus guessing weight, but I could see that eight wasn't going to cut it. "Are you sure you're not confusing that with eight kilograms?"

"Look, I was in the Cayman Islands this Spring, and I was diving with eight *pounds*."

He had either gained a lot or he was living in a state of denial. I gave him twelve.

Hans, the other instructor, was going to lead the first dive while I stayed on the boat. When the customers were in the water and ready, he gave the down signal. They deflated their BCs and everyone sank except for you know who. Small wonder. I handed Hans a five-pound weight and he slipped it into the guy's BC pocket, but our hero still bobbed like a cork. I handed over seven more pounds before he went under.

My agitation disappeared as I got comfortable on my captain's chair perch, prepared for forty minutes of lazy bubble watching. When the divers were fifty feet astern, the White Whale came flying up out of the water, feet-first. Moby had turned upside down, and the weights popped open his Velcro BC pockets. They fell to the sand as Archimedes' principle went into effect. While Hans tried to rectify the situation, my eyes narrowed behind my sunglasses, and I did my best Clint:

"Uh, uh. I know what you're thinking, punk. You're thinking, 'Did he put on six kilograms, or only five?' Now to tell you the truth, I've forgotten myself in all this excitement, but being how this is lead, the densest object on the boat, and will sink your ass clean to the bottom, you got to ask yourself one question: 'Do I feel buoyant?' Well, do ya . . . punk?"

Unfortunately, it got worse before it got better. On what normally would have been another beautiful day, an orca look-alike jumped off the boat (with a fully inflated BC), panicked the moment she got wet, and, fearing drowning, climbed the nearest available object, which was me. She got a firm grip on my hair, pushed me under, and held me there.

In this situation, my rescue course had taught me to push up on her, causing her to let go as I went further under water — but despite my efforts, she kept riding me like a beach ball. With my greatest wrestling performance since my junior-high championship, I was able to squirm around behind her and push her back to the boat. The crew, who had watched all this happen just out of reach, grabbed her tank valve and hauled her aboard like a net full of tuna.

On a lighter note, there was Herman the German, our largest student ever. With a wetsuit on, he set the men's weightbelt record at a whopping forty-five pounds. We didn't have a strap long enough to go around him, so the manager made a new one. Straight off the spool, this custom belt was seven feet long. (Keep in mind that forty-five pounds of molded lead eats up a lot of that length as the nylon strap weaves through.) Our next obstacle was that his rotund shape caused the belt to slide off his waist. Bandolier style made him lopsided, so he ended up wearing it around his chest. (This belt is still in use today, without the lead, holding the life raft onto the side of the dive boat.)

Herman only had one day off every week, so I ended up teaching a ten-week one-on-one dive course. As the season progressed and the water got warmer, we were able to lay aside his wetsuit and drop the belt down to twenty-eight pounds.

Unfortunately, some problems remained. Most divers with poor eyesight wear contact lenses or get masks with prescription lenses. Herman snapped the ear-hooks off an old pair of specs and stuck the frames inside. Then, after reading in his text about the importance of hand protection, he showed up to dive with a pair of pink rubber dishwashing gloves pulled up to his elbows. I wondered if he was trying to embarrass his instructor in front of the other staff. Hans loved to tease me, and Herman was giving him plenty of opportunities.

While we were tying up the boat one afternoon, Herman got excited, tried to step onto the dock too early, and missed. A brief instant of silence was followed by the sound of a very large splash between the boat and the pilings. Fortunately, the tide was in and the water was deep.

For his final dive, Herman displayed his prowess by cutting his head on the reef and getting tangled up in the anchor line of the boat. I gave him a Band-Aid along with his certification papers and sent him on his way. It wasn't until later, when life seemed dull around the dive shop, that we began to miss our fixture of weekly entertainment. Carry on, Herman, wherever you are.

COMBAT
Bermuda

"Maturity is a high price to pay for growing up." Tommy

Since our boat in Bermuda accommodated up to twelve divers, we split them into two groups. Hans would lead one bunch while I took the other. The dive sites were usually flat, so we wove various paths through the castle-like coral heads before returning to the anchored boat.

I don't know who started it, but every time we saw each other during a dive, Hans and I would draw imaginary six guns, wild-west style, and shoot it out. The loser would enact a grandiose dying scene, spitting out his regulator and sinking motionlessly.

We took the competition seriously. Whoever had the highest amount of kills for the day had bragging rights to the dive shop staff and girlfriends at home. We developed new ambush tactics, learning how to maneuver with a half-dozen divers tagging along. None of them had a clue what we were up to, and the shoot-outs happened so fast that surprisingly few people noticed. Once, Hans went so far as to swim out from the beach on his day off so he could massacre me while my guard was down.

As the summer progressed, our imaginary arsenal grew. We were soon shooting rifles, shotguns, Uzis, and bazookas. A really good kill was to sneak up behind the other guy and push a forefinger pistol barrel into the back of his neck. This was followed by the victim pleading for his life, a request always denied. We never took prisoners.

Near the end of the season, in murky conditions, I turned a corner and saw Hans swimming towards me, his attention directed off to the side. For this perfect ambush, I chose an M-16 on full auto. With my rifle raised, I inched closer, grinning like a wild man. As he looked up, I dumped the whole clip into his chest . . . but it wasn't Hans.

Embarrassed, I quickly disappeared, hoping the astonished customer hadn't recognized me. He never mentioned it, but his logbook might say, "Neat wreck. Bad visibility. Saw big grouper. Divemaster shot me."

THE CAVES
Bermuda

'The primitive beast that lingers within man has certain deep dreads, beyond logic, beyond intelligence. He dreads the dark. He fears being underground, which place he has always called the home of evil forces. He fears being alone. He dreads being trapped. He fears the water from which, in ancient times, he emerged to become Man. His most primitive nightmares involve falling through the dark, or wandering lost through mazes of alien chaos." Trevanian

"Experience is something you don't get until just after you need it." Anonymous

"You want to dive in *there*?" I looked skeptically at Hans.

"Best dive in Bermuda."

At the base of the limestone cliff was a pond thirty feet long by ten feet wide, surrounded by jungle. An oblong black void lay where the bottom should have been.

"Just remember the rule of thirds: 3,000 psi in the tank – a thousand in, a thousand out, and a thousand for your buddy if his regulator malfunctions. Stay close, and whatever you do, don't kick up any pond muck or the view will be screwed for the entire dive."

We eased ourselves down the rocks into the water, turned on our lights, and dropped through the hole. Even from a few feet away, a minor surge from my gentle finning had stirred up some loose clay from the edge of the pond. A muddy wisp rose and hung motionless as the water became still again. It would stay there for hours.

The entrance was a yawning chasm that angled down into darkness. Our flashlights illuminated forty-foot deep stalactites that once hung above sea level. After 200 feet of swimming, I saw why it was the country's best dive. From the distant entrance, the pond's surface projected images of the outside trees clearly enough for us to count each leaf. Black stalactite silhouettes dangled in the foreground – teeth along the upper edge of a mouth framing a surreal still life in green. A golden shaft of sunlight penetrated through the pond into the entrance. Its message to us was: We were saintly. We were privileged. We were alive, happily thriving in a silent realm.

Hans tapped my shoulder and pointed back into the darkness. We set our compasses and headed in. Ten minutes later, at the rear of the cave, we spotted light and surfaced in the air pocket under it. Fifty feet above, a fist-sized hole in the ceiling revealed green leaves and blue sky. Somewhere up on the jungle floor was a tiny, impossible to find, passage to our underworld.

☙ ☙ ☙

Three hundred yards down the trail from Hans' favorite cave was a gaping cavern with a high arched entrance. Inside, a ceiling rose up and away into dark air. The floor descended into shadowed water. On the west end, a string was tied off under water on a ten-foot deep stalagmite. Its taut white image headed northwest into blackness. Someone had been through there. Knowing what was on the other side of the ridge, I wondered how far back they had gone. Faced with the prospect of an exceptional adventure, I spent the next morning sweating and thrashing uphill through the jungle, compass in hand, to confirm my suspicions. When I emerged at the ridge top, I looked down to see a crowded parking lot adjoining the main road. The string in the cave was pointed directly towards the tourist cave.

I laid awake that night, dreaming up a personal fantasy scene in the tourist cave:

Fat kids eating candy clutch their mothers' hands with sticky fingers. The parents, sporting new knee length Bermuda shorts are locked in a permanent stoop from the weight of the cameras around their necks. The tour guide drones about geology with a Bermudian accent, "Rahnd a million years ago . . . " Suddenly, a bubble breaks the surface at the base of the colorfully lit flowstone. The guide whirls in amazement. More bubbles appear as a form moves under the surface. It's alive. Kids mash sugar into Daddy's polyester crotch as they cling for security. A hooded form appears. Mommy screams. A mass stampede breaks the wooden walkways as the drones flee to the safety of the tour bus.

I stand alone in the cave.

I am proud.

I didn't have to pay the seven-dollar entrance fee.

      ॐ   ॐ   ॐ

It was Tuesday, my day off, the day to explore the cave. Hans had to work, so I recruited Chris, another instructor on the island. Using a nautical chart, we carefully plotted a quarter mile course from the overhang cave to Tourist Central. In case of an emergency, we each carried an extra tank with regulator attached. In one gargantuan effort, we humped all of our equipment into the jungle at once.

Under the overhang, I looked at Chris's face beaded with sweat. "You look like you need to go for a nice cool dive."

"Let's go."

The string led down past narrowing gaps in the stalactites. Before losing view of the spot of light behind us, I gave it a tug to make sure it wouldn't break. Fifty feet later, we were squeezing through a narrow tunnel, churning up clay marl, and inching our way along the string in zero visibility. Finally, the passage opened, showing black water ahead. My light showed my bubbles tumbling up a wall to distant ripples, fifty feet above – an air pocket. I gave Chris the ascend signal.

At the surface, we inflated our BCs, and dropped our masks down. Forty feet above, a domed planetarium-like ceiling topped the circular underground room. In the reflections of our light beams, drops of groundwater shimmered in the dark where stars should have been. A gap in the opposite wall beckoned us to enter. We swam through the passage and emerged in a room the size of an indoor sports stadium. In the middle stood an island of glass-smooth ramps, formed by collapsed slabs from the ceiling. We took our gear off and scrambled to its summit.

"This is so cool." Chris's voice was dampened by the dripping white walls.

On the opposite wall, a half dozen more entrances indicated that there was a myriad of small passages leading north. However, none contained any caving line. The previous party had probably stopped where we stood.

"Let's go back and get a roll of kite string and check out these holes."

"All right."

Back in the planetarium room, we dropped back under water and followed the fifty foot contour to where we thought we came in. Nothing. No string. No tunnel. We searched all over the wall, but couldn't find the hole. We were trapped in the middle of Bermuda with the image of slowly dying from hunger in our minds. Hans and Monica knew where we went, but we could hardly sit in the dark hoping they would figure out where we were. We still had some air left plus the two extra tanks. We kept looking.

Fruitlessly our search expanded to areas we knew couldn't possibly hold the exit. On the east end of the slab room, we found another string, heading southeast. It was a dangerous proposition, but it appeared to be our best option. I gave Chris a "shall we?" shrug. He nodded. We followed it. After five anxious minutes of swimming, we began to make out a dim hint of light. A few moments later, we miraculously surfaced on the opposite end of the overhang cave. Plain old ordinary trees never looked so gorgeous. Their lively contrast to the dark dead zone behind brought us to a realization. There is nothing in underwater passages that can't be found in caves above sea level.

We never went back. Fun is one thing. Stupidity is another.

FISH FEEDING
Bermuda

"The only other thing I hate about this job is saltwater smear on my sunglasses." Hans

Spotting the shimmering image of someone leaning over a dive boat railing from under water is something I learned to do the hard way. As I approached the boat on scuba one morning, I was suddenly enveloped in somebody's breakfast. I dove back down and furiously combed my fingers through my hair to get the chunks out. Then I had to spend the day being reminded about it by Hans while he laughed.

Bermuda is a bad place for seasick-prone divers because it is in the middle of the Atlantic, unprotected from open ocean ground swells. I tell everyone who feels sick to go out on the deck and stare at the horizon. I make it clear that chundering on any part of the boat is a major social faux-pas and imply that anyone who even thinks about it will have something terrible happen to them. The only proper place to throw up is overboard and downwind. Boat crews have little patience for seasick divers who break this rule. Why? We're the ones who have to clean it up.

On what normally would have been another beautiful day, I had one delinquent pinhead insist on sitting inside the cabin as she got grayer and grayer. Five minutes later, she had the pallor of Marley's Ghost. I waved her out to the deck, but she refused. Ten minutes later, she finally lost it. To top things off, my favorite baseball hat bore the brunt of the attack. As I lifted my beloved cap into a bucket with a pencil and mopped up the mess, I muttered some bad, *bad* words. I can only hope that some horrible malady will befall her someday.

117

Later on in the summer, Hans was in the head after a dive, changing into dry shorts. A seasick customer raced for the toilet instead of going overboard. Fortunately for Hans, the door was locked. Unfortunately for Hans, he didn't suspect a thing. When he stepped out, his bare foot splashed in a puddle as he put his hand on the slimy doorknob. Revenge was sweet. It was my turn to laugh.

Enough on that subject.

YES, YOU TOO CAN DIVE
Bermuda

"Never argue with a fool. People might not know the difference." Anonymous

Step right up folks! Special today on diving. Sign up now for an introductory lesson and get ten percent off the cost of a full certification course. It's easy! It's fun! It's adventure! Learn how to dive in just one hour with our qualified instructors, and we'll have you out on the reef before you can say "bumphead parrotfish." All major credit cards are accepted. How about you, ma'am? Have you ever wanted to try diving?

Yes, but I don't know how to swim.

That's not a problem. Just sign here and come back at 12:30.

What about you, sir?

I've only got one leg.

That's okay. We'll throw in a fifty-percent discount on fin rental. Sign on the line, please. Thank you very much.

How about you, young lady? Would you like to visit our underwater wonderland? Everybody else is doing it.

Can I bring my dog?

Sure, no problem. Just sign here, and we'll see you at 12:30.

Anybody else? How about you there with the untied shoes?

Because Bermuda was only two hours by air from the East Coast, it drew a crowd with diverse interests. Many came for a week and chose an introduction to diving as one of their activities. This was instructor hell, because people who couldn't ride a bike without training wheels had access to the course. To complicate matters, our greedy dive shop owner packed the courses to the maximum limit and sometimes sent us out in rough seas, rainy weather, and horrid visibility. Keeping track of six novices we couldn't see in murky water was hell, but it taught us how to be great instructors in a hurry.

I had been spoiled badly by the exciting diving in Palau, and by the skill level of the divers that went there. In Bermuda, when I sat down at the end of the day to log my dives, I didn't find myself writing about exciting fish encounters. Instead, I filled up pages about the hilarious antics of beginning divers.

Diving isn't for everyone, and ten percent of the first-timers who tested their mettle quit before they even got out of the swimming pool. One woman took a few breaths on the regulator, decided we were all nuts, dumped off her gear in the shallow end and strode off. We never saw her again.

Peer pressure is a problem when enthused divers try to involve their uninterested spouses. The unwilling subjects often have trouble during the shallow water pool skills and stand up. I'll signal their partner to stay down, and then I'll go up for a one-on-one chat.

"If you really don't want to do this, you don't have to, you know."

"I thought you'd never ask. Can you create a diversion so I can sneak down to the beach?"

"Consider it done. Mask clearing is next so now is your chance."

"Thanks."

One dive goddess brought her boyfriend along on the boat and told everybody that she'd break up with him if he didn't learn to dive. I have never seen a man look so miserable under water. He let his weight belt pin him to the bottom, shuffled pathetically along on his knees through the sand, and almost started crying in his mask.

When I brought him to the surface, the girlfriend yelled over, "How was it for the first time?"

With a badly faked smile, the bold beau whimpered, "Wonderful, honey."

The things we do for love.

Another problem was divers with glasses. We didn't have prescription masks, so anyone without contact lenses had to dive with uncorrected vision. A middle aged woman clambered into the pool one afternoon and removed a pair of Coke-bottle specs. She couldn't see more than a foot, so I had to put my hand signals right in her face. She did well but realized it was pointless to go to the ocean without solving the problem. At the end of the lesson, she was fiddling around in the water by herself, removing and replacing her mask.

Curious, I asked, "What are you doing?"

"I can see better under water *without* a mask!"

One overeager American hit the water for his first dive and started kicking as hard as he could. I could barely keep up with him (it was just the two of us), so I signaled for him to slow down. Nothing. I yanked on his fins. Nothing. I tried tackling him, but he pressed on. Finally, I hauled him to the surface and pleaded with him to slow down. He nodded okay, shouted through his regulator, "This is great!" and bolted off again. I finally gave up, grabbed his high-pressure hose, and let him tow me around. After 22 minutes in 20 feet of water, we surfaced because he had used all his air.

Back on the beach, he raved, "That was great! That was really great! That was really fantastic!"

It wasn't bad for me either; I had an enjoyable ride and didn't have to swap my tank before the next dive.

Dale's first dive took up an entire logbook page when I wrote about him. Enthused, he also started kicking absently as soon as he hit the water. He reminded me of one of those little plastic divers that swim around kid's bathtubs; nothing could make him stop. The trick was to get him pointed in the intended direction of travel and let him go. Fortunately, his small fins and bicycling leg motions only produced a moderate underwater speed.

Ten minutes into his first dive, I looked back and saw him pointing excitedly at the reef. Normally when people do this, they have found a sea horse, octopus, moray, or something else that's fairly rare and interesting. I went back.

"What'd ya find, Dale?" I asked with a shrug.

The reef around him was flourishing with activity. Schools of fish darted past while others fish chased each other in fights for dominance. Lobster antennae protruded from crevices, wiggling. But Dale was pointing at a starfish, a creature that moved a hundred feet at most during the course of a day.

"That's great, Dale." I nodded to him reassuringly.

A few minutes later, he was waving again. I went back and lo and behold, there's another starfish. Okay, so the guy likes starfish. There's nothing wrong with that. Ten minutes later, he was gesticulating again, and Wow! A sea cucumber!

One afternoon, four typical students and a huge silent man came on the boat. His physique gave him away as someone who habituated weight rooms. At six-two, I was eye level with the middle of his chest. He was clean cut and looked tough as nails. My imagination made him out to be a trained killer for the military. I was afraid to ask.

After anchoring the boat, I helped the divers do their entries. He sat quietly in the corner and waited until last. After everybody else had gone into the water, he got up and threw his tank onto his back as if it were weightless. Without hesitation, he confidently strode out onto the dive platform and did a perfect entry.

Before I knew what was happening, he came flying up out of the water with all his equipment on, and again stood next to me. Silently dripping, he stared back down at the water.

I asked, "What's wrong?"

He replied in a soft high voice, "I'm frightened."

I had to bite my tongue to keep from laughing. You can never tell by looking.

That night, I wrote down the story of "The Big Guy" in my logbook and looked back through the hundreds of dives I had already done in Bermuda. There were a lot of funny stories in there and some included the staff of the dive shop . . .

STUPID INSTRUCTOR TRICKS
Bermuda

"There is no substitute for experience." Darius

We are dive gods, perfect in every way. The boat's bridge is our throne and the sea our domain. Dozens of innocents entrust us daily with their lives. *Bravado* goes with the territory. By mid-season, we function flawlessly during our work routine . . . almost. (The following stories *never happened.*)

I soar into work on a mountain bike, giving everybody in the shop a happy good morning wave as the front tire drops between the wooden slats of the pier. Seven somersaults later, I'm clinging to the edge, trying not to drop onto the rocks below. Why people laugh at this is something to ponder. Doing a high-speed faceplant into a splintery pier isn't funny — it's painful.

An unlashed gangplank balances freely between the pier and the floating dock. At seven-thirty in the morning, Hans stumbles sleepy-eyed down the ramp. One of the boat boys pulls the starter cord on a Boston Whaler that was left in gear at full throttle. The engine catches and races, pulling the dock slowly out to sea. Hans' lethargic stride pauses as his sleep addled brain realizes that something more important than the coffee cup in his hand is going to effect his immediate existence. His jaw falls as his eyelids snap open. With one gargantuan leap, he manages to get airborne as the gangplank drops into the water. Miraculously he lands on the edge of the dock, spilling only a few drops of coffee in the process. Now *that's* funny.

I'm docking the boat. Hans jumps ashore with the stern line. I pop the gearshift up into neutral and jump off the bridge for the bow line. My shorts catch the shift lever, ramming the boat into forward at full throttle. I'm hanging off the bridge by my shorts — a figurehead in full wedgie position. My momentary destination is through the windows of the dive shop ahead. I cover my face with my arms and prepare for impact. Inches before the boat launches over the sea wall, it lurches to a halt. Hans has managed to belay my antics with the stern line. I disengage my backside, grateful that no one else is watching. Hans demands hush money. I pay up.

REVERIE
Bermuda

"Life is too short to put up with a bad climate." Alan

Crystal-blue solitary void of water. Fish cluster around an algae-covered circus tent far below. Down to it alone — deep, deep, deep. Narcosis takes control of my senses, transporting me into an ethereal realm as I reach the thriving sanctuary. I survey the netting. A long slit beckons me to explore. Brushing the fish aside, I part it and enter the chamber. Blue is replaced by green. I ignore a white metal sundeck chair that has fallen from a passing boat as I enter the nursery. Every known marine species offers a touching welcome as I wander among them, experiencing true inner peace. The tepid water caresses my skin. Happy warmth in my belly spreads throughout my body. I smile in my regulator and shut my eyes.

I awake without a scuba tank in a utopian fairyland. Divers wander blissfully about the depths. I join them. Finning playfully, I skirt the coral heads with the grace of a seal. Every so often, I remind myself to drop by for a gracious breath from someone's spare regulator before continuing my exhilarating sojourn.

I swim to the caves in the cliff ahead, and as I pass the office at the entrance, I wave at the two clerks lazily reading newspapers. They smile and wave back. A dark shaft drops downward. The bottom glows hundreds of feet below. I go deeper. The light intensifies as I enter the tunnel system near the bottom. Stopping to take a breath in an air pocket is necessary before pushing onward. I venture confidently in for a visit to the embryonic Nirvana ahead. I have been there before, but when?

125

The chambers are backlit like swimming pools at night. I wander through the aquatic dream world to the room where the grouper dwells. He's waiting in his usual spot. As always, he lets me rub the backs of my knuckles against his lips before disappearing into his inky black hole. On my way out, I stop at the office to report that I have discovered two new passages to put on the map. Then I go home.

I rolled over and stared at the sunlight on Monica's empty side of the bed. The familiar limy aroma of Bermudian whitewash wafted through the open window. A stinky hint of mildew escaped from the pillow. What day was it? My day off. Good. I could go play golf. Grabbing a towel to wear, I lumbered over to the bathroom and peed without closing the door.

When I finished, I wandered out to the kitchen. Monica paused her eating motion halfway to her mouth. A careless drop of milk fell from the Corn Chex in her spoon back to the bowl. It splashed quietly, sending a tiny white driblet out onto the wooden table.

She shook her head at my bedraggled appearance. "How were your dreams?"

"Great. Why?"

"You were wiggling your toes and blowing bubbles in your sleep. Were you diving?"

"Big time."

I plucked a clean cup out of the dish rack and headed for the half-full pot in the coffee maker.

Monica ate her Chex.

LA DANIA'S LEAP
Bonaire

"Diving is as safe as you want to make it." Frank

Pay for diving? Not if I can help it. That's my job. If I do have to pay, it's going to be as little as possible. I had scrounged my way through America's national parks on climbing trips for only a few dollars a day. All I had to do was apply those principles to scuba. No problem. When Monica and I got to Bonaire, a Caribbean island off the coast of Venezuela, we became dive bums for a week. While hundreds of other divers were tucked comfortably in resorts on thousand-dollar dive packages, we were sleeping in a rented mini-van. When they relaxed in their hot tubs, we showered under the hose behind the dive shop. Where their dive boats dropped them off at the sites, we trudged in from the beach and swam out.

The reefs of Bonaire began just offshore and quickly dropped from ten feet to a hundred and forty — perfect for long deep profiles. We started at the base of them every morning, substituting nitrogen narcosis highs for coffee. We enjoyed the way the reef characteristics changed with depth; every animal had its niche. Visibility was invariably outstanding due to the island's lack of streams (which dump silt into the sea, clouding the water).

The mini-van was the ultimate dive vehicle. Its short turning radius was ideal for back-road assaults on the profusion of dive sites ringing the island. The bare metal floor behind the two front seats held our equipment during the day and our tired bodies at night. Tanks were rented from one of the local shops for next to nothing. They bounced through the tire ruts with us as we passed cactus and flamingos along the way.

The desolate nights of Bonaire provided ideal bivouac conditions. Nobody drove around after dark, so sleep and privacy were undisturbed. The van wasn't a bad place to sleep, but after two nights of rocking around in high winds, we moved into the slave huts south of town. They were low stone structures built for the salt miners of the last centuries, and many were refurbished by the government to attract tourists. I don't know if anyone actually made sightseeing trips to them, but they looked good on postcards, and provided us with great shelter.

One night in a seaside pub, we were seated beside a bunch of male boozers speaking Papamiento, the local dialect. A few of them didn't have chairs and were standing. I was distracted in conversation with some divers behind me when Monica stood up to watch the waves for a few minutes. When she went to sit back down, she almost fell because her seat was gone. Somebody from the next table had snatched it.

"Excuse me. Can you please return my chair?"

The drunken slobs clearly heard, but ignored her.

She exploded. "Hey, if you want a chair you should ask. Not just take one from somebody who isn't looking. Now, give me back my chair!"

The dumpiest looking thug said, "Shut up, bitch."

That brought me into it. I stood up and pointed at him. "Watch your mouth."

Their whole table jumped up, and the bar went quiet except for the music. I was bigger than all of them but was outnumbered eight to one. Men all around us were also getting ready to leap into the action. I had a clear shot at the jaw of the closest goon, but held back, knowing I'd probably get my ass handed to me. The attention shifted back to Monica as she unleashed a verbal tirade. They wouldn't take a swing at a woman in a crowded bar, so I stepped back and let her go. Finally, a waiter materialized with a chair, and it was over. We sat back down.

The next morning at the dive shop, I was loading tanks into the mini-van when one of the divemasters gave me an uncommonly big smile. "Hey, you did all right last night."

"You saw that? Sorry about the commotion."

"No, no. Don't worry about it. Those idiots are from Curaçao. We hate those bastards here. They're always coming over and starting trouble."

Now he tells me. The other guys in the bar had been on *our* side.

కీ కీ కీ

Some of Bonaire's dive sites were located below limestone cliffs and accessible only by boat. The exception was La Dania's Leap, a twenty-foot high overhang above a boulder-free section of shoreline. The trick was to park at a nearby cove, don all equipment, walk down the rocky cliff tops, do a "giant stride" over the precipice, and then swim back.

After humping our loads down to the entry point, we stopped and surveyed the "leap." Whenever incoming waves impacted the base of the cliff, the rock shuddered and spray flew overhead. The water level would rise almost to the our feet before dropping suddenly to expose the reef below. If our jumps were poorly timed, we would be smashed into the coral, shredded along it, and then mangled into unique new shapes against the base of the wall. The only possible departure time was when the water was at its highest. Once in, the trick was to swim like hell out to sea before the next upsurge.

Monica was the perfect dive girlfriend. Once again, she was joining me on one of my wilder adventures. When we arrived at the leap, she wanted to jump first. Her fin tips hung out into space as she fastened a hand over her mask and regulator. When the next big swell powered in, I waited until the spray flew past, then gave an extra shove to her tank as she plunged in. Through foam-free gaps in the turmoil, I could see the colors of her neon wetsuit getting wooshed out over the reef.

When the next rush of water barreled in, I didn't see any sign of her. That meant that she was waiting for me at thirty feet as planned. I launched forward into the water and fell with it as the enormous Maytag torrent rushed out. The pause between the

129

drain and rinse cycles was just long enough to let me swim out over the edge.

When I got down next to Monica, she took out her reg and mouthed, "Wow." I nodded in agreement as we started off in the direction of the exit cove. It took a few minutes to calm down before we began to notice the finer features of the reef. Something caught my eye so I tapped Monica and swam over to investigate. An octopus was stretched to the size of a bowling ball over a dead fish. Against the surrounding sand, its camouflage made it nearly invisible. We moved in slowly, but it spooked, let go of the fish, shrunk to the size of a Coke can, and fled to a nearby hole under a rock, changing color again to match the gray.

I took the fish over and laid it in front of the hole while the cephalopod warily kept an eye on us. After a minute, it reached out and grabbed the fish with a suckered arm. I grabbed the tail, and started a game of tug of war, amazed at how strong it was. Next, I pulled the fish away and laid my hand on the doorstep. After a minute, it reached out and sucked down hard enough on my skin to make me flinch. I tried again a few times, but no matter how hard I concentrated, I couldn't override my body's natural reaction to recoil. Then I put my hand down too close, and the octopus picked up dozens of rocks and shells in its tentacles and held them up to make a barrier across the front of the hole. The wall looked as if it were cemented in place. Game Over.

While we drifted back the distance we had schlepped on foot, Monica's air got low. We stayed under by having her ride on my tank while breathing on my spare. At the cove exit, she replaced her own reg before crawling with me out through the surf on hands and knees.

"That was such a great dive!"

"Wasn't that awesome?"

Fins in hand, we trudged up the steep track.

When we got to the parking lot, my heart missed a beat. One of the van windows had been pried open. I immediately opened the door and checked for our valuables. My ratty duct-taped money belt was intact, but Monica wasn't so lucky. The thief had found her more attractive stash under the seat and made off with her wallet, jewelry, passport, credit cards, and plane tickets. We were screwed. I only had a hundred dollars in cash left, and Bonaire didn't have a British embassy. Even if we had money wired to us, there was no way to get her home to Bermuda without a passport. Could we get through by pleading with immigration officials? Doubtful. Could I fly out, get everything for her, and come back? She had to be back at work in four days. In shock, we drove the mini-van into town and found the police headquarters.

Inside, the only officer on duty lounged behind a desk in standard siesta mode. As we related our shocking news, he gazed languidly under drooping eyelids and scribbled a few sentences on a report form. He mentioned that the thief was probably on foot, because the rare criminal in Bonaire was usually a druggie bum who didn't own a car. Other than that, he couldn't offer any helpful advice whatsoever. We said thanks and left him to carry on with his nap.

After hearing about the bush bums, Monica had a brainstorm. She wondered aloud if the thief had ditched the non-valuable stuff near the crime scene. Maybe we could find something that at least proved who she was.

Back at the parking lot, we split up to scour the scrub brush. After thirty minutes of thrashing through the overgrowth, we hadn't found a thing. I was tired of fording thickets in the hot sun so I yelled over to Monica that we weren't accomplishing anything. She pleaded with me, so I resumed the search.

After an hour, I found an old purse. Inside was a cosmetic case, a driver's license, and some old credit cards. I let out a shout.

Monica's voice, far away in the chaparral, asked excitedly, "Did you find it?"

"No, but it looks like thieves have dumped stuff here before. Keep looking!"

I plunged back into the hunt with fervor.

Ten minutes later, Monica screamed, "I found my passport!"

As I tumbled through the brush in the direction of her voice, she screamed again. "I found my credit cards, I found my plane tickets!"

"Where were they?"

"Under some rocks."

I was blown away. The only thing she lost was her jewelry and a small amount of cash.

What a day. There was nothing left to do but dive, but what site should we choose?

La Dania's Leap was so great the first time, we went back and did it again — this time with our valuables hidden under some cactus.

BIG JOHN
Antigua

"When you can't peel a banana anymore, it's time to go home." Chris

At the end of the dive season in Bermuda, I met the owners of the Wanderer IV, Eric Hiscock's famous forty-nine foot ketch. They were headed for New Zealand by way of Panama and offered me a crew position as far as Antigua. Finally, I had the chance to go *down island* to the real Caribbean.

We left Saint George's Harbour on Halloween, headed due south on a starboard reach. The striated sunset showed only two colors — black and orange. As a full moon rose, the candle in our carved pumpkin flickered haphazardly in the cockpit. The Bermuda lighthouses bid us a blinking farewell before disappearing over the horizon. I was on a boat that wouldn't stop rocking and headed for a land that never got cold.

The weather was mild, which was perfect for comfort, but not speed (not that sailboats are fast in the first place). I spent the midnight watches nestled atop a sail bag on the bow while the autopilot lazily steered a course of one-eight-zero. The waning moon emerged nightly from the edge of the sea, masking the dome of stellar pinpoints with a chalky cloud. On the ninth night, a glow materialized above the horizon off the starboard bow — the lights of Antigua. A fresh gust sprung out of the east and the ketch buried her starboard rail into the sea. As it sliced the backs of the waves, green phosphorescence flickered down the deck next to the portholes. The knotmeter read 7.5 — a good clip for the old Winnebago.

In the morning, we sailed past a cliff-top lighthouse and put in at English Harbour, renowned yacht haven of the Caribbean. The bay was remarkably situated under towering hills. Behind, a

133

restored English fort housed a museum and an array of tourist shops. A thick chain, once slung across the mouth of the bay, prevented the intrusion of masted enemy vessels. It was lowered to allow English ships through and supported by stanchions that could still be seen.

An old crew member had flown in to meet the boat, so I had two choices — get a job and stay, or go back to California. It wasn't a hard decision. When I started asking around for work as a diving instructor, a local divemaster gave me the number of a Danish shop owner named Big John. I went to the phone. Big John answered. After a brief chat, he asked me to come up to his dive shop for an interview the next day at noon.

In the morning, I shaved and dug my best shirt out of my sea bag. Big John's business was located on the other end of the island at a large resort. I took public transportation as far as I could and then hitchhiked the rest of the way. In the lobby, I asked about the shop and was directed to the far end of the beach. I trudged through the sand to find an old building with scuba tanks lying against the side of it. It was locked. Nailed to the roof was a huge sign that read, BIG JOHN'S DIVING ADVENTURES. I took a seat and waited. My watch said noon.

On the sand in front of the shop was an incredible array of European women using the end of the beach to sunbathe naked. There was no sign of John, so I put my feet up and ogled. Twenty minutes later, a huge long-haired blonde-bearded Viking drifted up the beach with a half-gallon bottle of rum and a bag of ice in his hands. I watched, transfixed, as he wandered right up to me. His extra large T-shirt was stretched to capacity. Printed across the front was "Big John."

As he came in, he nodded toward the women. "I pay the hotel extra to send 'em up here."

He tossed the ice on the table and set the bottle next to it.

"Hi, I'm Mike." I stood and held out my hand for a handshake.

He slapped an empty plastic cup into it. "I think this one's pretty clean. There're Cokes in the cooler. Fix us some drinks while I open up."

Wanting to make a good impression, I tore open the ice bag and mixed a couple strong ones. He looked like the type that preferred 'em that way.

The gregarious Dane tossed drinks back one after another as he rambled on about everything except scuba diving. Four hours and a hell of a lot of Antiguan rum later, the sun was getting low. When the last nude put her clothes on and wandered away, he finally got down to business by asking to see my resume. After glancing over it, he invited me to go out the next day. He nodded towards the boat on the offshore mooring. Painted across the transom of the craft were the words "Big John."

Dive shop interviews typically involve a day of diving, and a prospective employee tries to help out as much as possible. After loading the boat the next morning and shuttling the customers in the dinghy, I was off to the open ocean on the SS Big John. The first dive site was located in the shoals that stretched for miles to the west of the island. It was named Big John's Place and he used a satellite navigation system to find it. When we were ready to dive, John said, "Follow me, I think you'll like this." I brought up the rear as he led his half dozen customers around in an interesting way. Every fifty feet or so, he would stop and write marine biology facts on his slate and then point to a living example. The customers loved it.

The last stop on the dive was a shelf next to a sandy bowl. Big John wrote "Nurse Shark" on his slate and motioned for us to look over the edge. I jumped back in surprise when I saw a twelve-foot monster staring at me from two feet away. Big John motioned for me to pet it, so I imitated him by gently running my fingers along the sandpaper skin. Shark skin feels smooth when rubbed toward the tail, but rougher than a five o'clock shadow in the direction of the head. The shark didn't mind being petted by a horde of strange looking creatures – probably because Big John did this several times a week. After we finished playing with it, Big John pointed under another ledge. Hidden in the crevice was another nurse shark, nine feet long.

Back on the boat, Big John showed us fragments of lemon-sized cowrie shells. He explained that the nurse sharks feed on them and other hard-to-eat bottom dwellers, including lobsters. Besides being educational, this comforted anyone who had been worried about them being man-eaters.

The second locale was Little Big John's, leaving me wondering what the other sites were named. Halfway through the dive, something wiggling in the sand caught my eye. I looked down to see an almond-sized cowrie emerging slowly to the surface of the sand. The shape of its unhurried trajectory reminded me of a dolphin leaping forward in slow motion. As it was disappearing back into the sand, a wrasse shot in and knocked the cowrie flying shell-over-ventral-foot. As soon as the little guy was upside down, the wrasse nipped a hunk out of its flesh and swam off. The crippled cowrie took a minute to recover, then carried on with its burrowing descent.

Then I noticed a goatfish chewing vigorously on something. After awhile, it gave up and spit it out. The object was a small clam that the goatfish had dug out of the sand with its "whiskers." Clam 1, Goatfish 0. Despite their protective covering, shells have it tough.

After pondering molluskan existence, I joined the contented customers on the boat. Big John broke out a fresh bottle of the same locally distilled rum I had gotten to know the day before and had me mixing drinks for everyone. By the time the boat got back, I was riding a terrific buzz.

Big John asked, "Would you like to go out with the resort divers this afternoon?"

"I'm feeling kind of hammered."

He laughed. "Don't worry, you don't have to do anything, just follow them around and see how the operation runs."

So off I went for an hour under water with the new guys. Every breath from my regulator filled my sinuses with the smell of booze – the longest cocktail I ever tasted.

I never got the chance to work with Big John again because I found a better-paying job in Saint Lucia. I regretted passing up the opportunity, but my liver was grateful.

WINDING
Saint Lucia

"What men call gallantry and gods adultery,
Is much more common where the climate's sultry." Byron

The only good thing about living in the little fishing village of Soufriere was the lack of racial tension. Three dive instructors lived among the residents of the all-black town. Tourists rarely stayed there, so the foreign population was usually just us. After living in Oakland, California, where a few friends of mine had their asses kicked for being white, I found the harmony of Soufriere refreshing.

The town was isolated in a valley bottom by high volcanic hills on three sides. The famous Pitons – volcanic plugs that shot 2,500 feet up out of the sea, provided a sublime backdrop to the south. Soufriere was picturesque from nearby hilltops, but dilapidated and dirty up close.

A potholed four-wheel-drive road served as the only land access to our secluded workplace in the next bay. Forested bluffs jutted straight up on either side of the beach. Between them, a sharp ridge rose from the water's edge, dotted with resort cabanas that reminded me of Disneyland's Swiss Family Robinson tree house. Majestic and finished in wood, many rooms had living tree trunks growing through the middle of them. Each was unique in design, and every verandah's panorama was unobstructed and private (one of the reasons that the hotel was a favorite for honeymooners).

Of the three of us, I was the new guy. Freddy was from Florida and had been there several months longer than I had. He was hired by phone on a year contract without having been to the island. After expecting to live in posh resort conditions, the reality of living in the shabby town did a daily dive bombing run of his lower emotions. The course of this emotional strafing got so low that he finally dropped off the radar. When I met him, he brooded all day without talking to anyone, dwelling on what he missed most – his friends, family, and everything else that he had going on in the States.

I started to feel the same way after awhile, often referring to Soufriere as the Deliverance town of the Caribbean, and it wasn't just the fifty-percent literacy rate, rampant nose picking, and crotch digging in public that made me say that. Olfactory assaults slapped out from anyone passing within three feet because underarm deodorant was too expensive. People threw bags of garbage into the creek and treated domestic animals worse than houseflies. Displaced from their native cultures for hundreds of years, they had lost touch with humanity's guidelines for manners.

Klaus, the other instructor, had been there for years. He was great to work with – helpful, cheerful, and never down. Despite the obvious drawbacks, which he blindly accepted, he was enraptured with Saint Lucia. He learned the local patois (French dialect) and visited his beautiful local girlfriend on his day off. He made good money, did not have to endure German winters, and loved life. He had ready-made speeches for Freddy and me on how to survive Saint Lucia and lectured us several times a week. We listened, but there wasn't much we could do. Fishing village life just wasn't our gig.

There was nothing to do at night except read our paperbacks from home or drink. We chose to drink. Every night found us holding down a corner of Tata's rum shop. Tata was a middle-aged woman of Indian descent who blended with the rest of the Saint Lucians only slightly better than us white boys. From behind the bar, she participated in every conversation and functioned as the fulcrum of our micro-community; her shop was our home away from home.

The rum shop was a concrete cinder-block room with dim lighting. Long benches ran down the inside walls, and rickety tables were set parallel to them. A multicolored assortment of plastic and wooden chairs wandered around the bare floor, and the walls were adorned with pastel paint and rum posters featuring Caribbean knockouts in bikinis. A wooden bar was set against the back wall, and the open door behind led straight into the living room of Tata's adjacent house.

The urinal was simply the cinder block wall in the alley next to the entrance. A four-foot-high rusty gate provided semi-privacy from the street while we relieved ourselves on the gray bricks. Occasionally, someone would write their name for fun, reliving childhood stunts, or showing off dexterous capabilities to the next visitor. Below the wall, a gutter drained the artwork over to the open trench next to the sidewalk.

The crowd, other than the three of us, consisted mostly of regulars – our best buddies away from the dive shop. Rum flowed freely between the tables and was portioned out in nips, old hip flasks filled from a 750ml bottle through a funnel. A full bottle of Saint Lucian rum was about three bucks, and the nip prices were proportionate. Coke mixers were thirty cents. The ice was free. As glasses got empty, whoever was feeling the most generous would get the next round. The empties piled up and the ice supply dwindled. Everybody was at least jovial if not gregarious by the end of every night.

Trying to make friends with the rest of the villagers wasn't as easy. We weren't celebrities, but we weren't treated badly either. There was some impenetrable gap that we couldn't quite cross. However, we did slide into the culture unobtrusively at the local "dance hall."

The disco was small and dark, and everyone knew whenever it was open because the Dub music it blared could be heard throughout the town. Dub is a Caribbean non-melodic driving bass beat with Reggae somewhere in its ancestry. The dance that is done to Dub would be illegal in most countries and is called Winding (pronounced "wine-in"). Here's how it goes: Single women dance alone on the floor, gyrating their butts wildly and bending at the knees limbo style to wind down to the floor and back up. If that by itself doesn't make the point, some will place their palms on the floor to emphasize their butt wiggles. Many also lean back at times and gently pinch and hold their clitorises through the fabric of their pants with their thumb and forefinger splayed out as if they're daintily holding a teacup. To dance, a man simply walks up behind a woman on the floor, grabs her hips, places his groin against her butt, and winds with her. I couldn't imagine trying this with a beautiful woman in an all-black club in Oakland. If I did, I doubt they'd ever find my body parts.

A couple times in the disco, men tried to pimp women to me.

Once, I played along and asked, "What woman?"

The guy said, "That one, right there, for twenty dollars."

"What does she think about that?"

"Just a second. I'll ask."

He walked over and said something in her ear. She slapped him hard across the face.

He came back over and said, "Sorry, she's not going for it."

"Does she normally work as a whore?"

"No, She's my sister."

Anything for a buck, I guess.

&❧ &❧ &❧

The Saint Lucian divemasters were supposed to work eight-to-four, provide customer service, and clean up the shop when not under water. In reality, they appeared ten minutes before one of the dives, yawning and wiping sleep from their eyes. After the dives, they'd disappear, and we'd be stuck with their chores.

Klaus filled me in on the history of the divemaster hideaways: Years before, when the new American manager took over, the first thing he did was have the impromptu beds in the compressor room removed. The next day, he noticed that the chickens clattering on the tin roof had gained a lot of weight. He went outside, looked up, and found a divemaster dragging a mattress up. This was also disallowed, so the boys headed for the banana trees with their foamys. The manager started going into the jungle on search and destroy missions, but this only drove them deeper. The hidden lairs are there to this day.

One morning, Klaus came in laughing. "Hey, come out here. You guys have to see this." Less than a hundred feet from the dive shop was the storage shed for beach activities. Behind the windsurfing sails was a partially overturned dinghy. A fully reclined beach chair had ingeniously been slipped underneath. If it hadn't been for loud snoring coming out, Klaus never would have found it.

$$\approx \quad \approx \quad \approx$$

After twenty years in Saint Lucia, the English maintenance man at the resort was a walking zombie, refusing to speak with anyone who hadn't been there for at least a year. Following his jeep up the four-wheel drive road to work one morning, we watched several quarts of gasoline slosh out of his capless tank. The spilling stopped at the top of the hill, but the oil drain plug fell out as he started down the grade to the resort, leaving a mile-long sludge streak in the dust. He was oblivious to both problems.

It was time for me to leave. I had to get out of there before I ended up like him.

KNOW YOUR ENEMY
Saint Lucia

"'. . . we'll describe everything as the eye of God might see it. We'll tell about the beauty, yes, but we'll also speak honestly of the desolate bitterness.' He was well now and became excited, for he wanted to narrate the simple truths of island life." Michener

"Necessity is the mother of invention." Jonathan

Chickens belong in coops. It is beyond me why people in the tropics allow these nuisances to freely roam their neighborhoods. My village in Saint Lucia had chickens everywhere — and not just normal chickens, but loud demonic chickens with bad timing. Some crowed through the night. The rest woke up before sunrise to join in, driving me out of my mind as I tossed and turned, trying to sleep.

One big black rooster had a favorite spot in the tree next to my bedroom window. Every night around midnight, he would flutter noisily into his roost and announce his virility with a bloodcurdling 100-decibel off-key screech that made him sound like he was being garroted. Anticipating his next shriek prevented me from getting back to sleep.

I showed up for dives with bags under my eyes. Throbbing headaches made the daylight hours as miserable as the nighttime. After work, I tried to catch some shut-eye, but this was when my neighborhood was loudest. Dogs barked, pigs snorted, children screamed, cars revved, stereos blared, people shouted, and the metal shop across the street did grinding work. Above all, there was the incessant background squawking of the chickens. The only escape was to flee to the rum shop and join the other instructors until closing time.

It was time for war, so the next time the critter announced himself, I tore out into the dark yard in my underwear and fired a rock into the tree. This only made the ornery cretin go silent and hold still. I couldn't see him in the thick leafy limbs, but I could sense his beady glare coming defiantly out of the darkness. Seething, I hurled sticks, chunks of concrete, and anything else lying on the ground into the branches, but the tenacious bird wouldn't budge an inch. I had no choice but to go back to bed and endure more of his vicious outbursts.

I wondered if he was mentally retarded for not retreating to a more peaceful hangout until I realized the truth: It was ingrained in his rooster genes to be indefatigable in the face of combat. The pea-brained little guerrilla would fiercely hold his ground until one of us went down for the count. The battle of wills was on.

The next day, I borrowed a slingshot and waited up. When he fluttered into position, I stepped out, drew the rubber sling back to my chin, and sent a rock sizzling through the leaves. My foe flapped away, unscathed, but was back fifteen minutes later. Once again, I put a high-speed missile past his head. Again he fled, but returned as soon as things quieted down. As I gave up a second time, I could feel him looking down his beak at me.

My pitiful attacks made him cockier, so to speak. The next morning, he followed me down the road as I went to work, cocka-doodle-doo-ing taunts at me. As soon as I got to the dive shop, I grabbed a fiberglass sail batten and slotted a section of hacksaw blade into the tip. Using the slingshot as a bow, I test fired it into a coconut. While working it out of the husk, a trickle of coconut milk leaked out. My face twisted into a fiendish grin as an inborn sensation from my primal past coursed through my blood. I could now match his ruthlessness on the battlefield.

Envisioning chicken shish kebabs, I filed the saw blade down until it was razor sharp. When my oppressor arrived that night, I was waiting. Adrenaline coursed through my veins as I crept catlike out to the tree. I probed the darkness with my eyes but was unable to see anything except shadowed branches and leaves. Then one of the silhouettes fluttered slightly.

Oooh, Yes. Come to Papa, sweetheart.

Range: six feet.

Bearing: zero eight seven.

Elevation: seventy-three degrees.

I drew the arrow back in the slingshot and raised the tip into imaginary cross hairs. I exhaled slowly and released. The steel blade made a thwacking sound as it entered his breast. He fluttered wildly until the arrow dropped out and then escaped over the wall. I was convinced he was going off to die somewhere.

I curled up happily in my sheets, but when I reached the dreamy brink of slumber, I heard it in the distance, "Bruk, Bruk, Bruk, Bruk, BaBruk . . . Bruk, Bruk-Bruk."

After a short pause, another chicken replied, "Bruk, Bruk-Bruk, Bruk, Bruk . . . Bruk, BaBruk."

I had understood what they were saying! They were talking about what a son-of-a-bitch I was. Had I gone completely nuts? Either way, the good news was, enemy communications had been intercepted and decoded.

Two hours later, I found out that my dusky companion was the Schwarzenegger of roosters. The incorrigible little shit not only lived, he came back. I had to up the firepower in a big way.

Pursuing a devilish inspiration, I dug around the dive shop for the necessary scraps. I discovered that used outboard roller bearings could be rammed down a high-pressure compressor hose with a coat hanger. Oh, he was in for it now. With a scuba tank and a snap valve, I could instantly put 3,200 psi of pressure behind the steel bullets. I let a few test shots fly out over the reef, then straightened the hose into a barrel by taping a windsurfing batten to it. Impending victory became a reality as I added a narrow beamed Pelican light to the barrel configuration. The idea was to put the light beam on the target, then, BLAMMO. Preliminary tests with the X-weapon proved that it could easily put a hole in a piece of wood paneling. I couldn't wait to see what it would do to a chicken.

On my way home that night, scuba tank over my shoulder, rooster-loving neighbors asked me if I was going night diving.

"Yes," I lied.

When the little black bastard rocked me out of bed, I calmly slid my arms through the backpack straps of the X-weapon and crept quietly out the back door. He saw me tip-toeing up to the tree and held as still as he could. After my eyes adjusted to the darkness, I searched the crisscrossing silhouettes of branches above me. One of them had a beak. When I turned the Pelican light on, the smug son of a bitch froze like a deer caught in the headlights. I had him. I readied the release hand, and concentrated. A quick snap of the wrist was essential for maximum firepower, but I had to be careful not to jerk the barrel as I shot. I put the center of the beam on his torso and let off a beauty. The Fowl of Darkness let out a hell of a squawk and fluttered away. I couldn't tell if the bearing had gone into him or just bounced off. Either way, he was damn tough!

The X-weapon was loud as hell in the still night. I laid low in the bushes until I thought my neighbors had gone back to sleep, then slinked back into my house. I didn't need it again that night because the black rooster was gone for good. Victory was finally mine. Yes!

Two nights later, I could hear familiar squawking in the distance. Damn. It was him. He was far enough away for me to sleep, but we both knew that could change at any second. I set up a listening post in the living room to track his movements. I got a fix on his position and dialed in on his conversation. John Rambo Rooster was rallying his comrades by screaming, "He drew first blood! He drew first blood!" Now I'd done it. I had incurred the wrath of every feathered miscreant in the neighborhood. If I showed the slightest sign of weakness, they would overrun my perimeter.

The X-weapon tipped the balance of power in my favor. Without it, my peck-marked body would be found after not showing up to work. Unfortunately, the neighbor factor kept me from taking countermeasures behind enemy lines.

It got to the point where I could hear every subtle noise coming from the other side as they hopped, scratched, and fluttered about. They probed my defenses one at a time, and at odd intervals. I couldn't wear the X-weapon around all the time, so I readied a backup arsenal for retaliatory strikes from anywhere inside my redoubt. In the first barricade of the living room, the slingshot stood at ready next to used Walkman batteries and off-caliber roller bearings. Sharp rocks adorned the top of my refrigerator. A dive knife was stabbed into the wood of the bathroom doorjamb in case I got caught with my pants down.

On three sides of the command post bedroom, I removed glass plates from each of the louvered windows. With the ability to shoot in every direction, I suppressed every hint of invasion by taking potshots at any chicken in range. After a shot, my neighbors would occasionally come out to see what the ruckus was, but they could never pin it on me. Who could they suspect? I was hidden inside my fort. Who would believe it, anyway?

Freddy and I preserved each other's sanity by freely venting our woes in the rum shop, but the bleary bull sessions took their toll. A tropical depression struck. Klaus was bluntly unsympathetic to us in his austere Bavarian way. When I complained about the chickens, he replied, "So what? They don't bother the locals. Why are you upset?" For someone who had blended into the culture so well, Mister Holier than Thou had nothing better to do than waste his evenings drinking with us, didn't he?

My daylight hours were occupied with entertaining tourists on the beautiful 300-foot dropoff in front of the hotel beach. Conversations with them reminded me that there was a real world out there. I could joke, have fun, and forget that I had to go home at the end of each day, wile away the evening with two fellow drunks, and plot the demise of certain species of fowl.

One night in bed, after a full-on rum session, I lost it. I could hear the chickens out at the area perimeter, defiantly making a racket. Cluck-cluck bruk-bruk cock-a-doodle-doo seemed to be a personal attack on none other than *moi*. I smoldered at their insouciance, and wished the X-weapon had greater range. Finally, I leaped drunkenly out of bed and started screaming, "Shut up! Shut up, you little bastards or I'll wrench your fucking heads off!" When my alarm went off in the morning, I woke up and winced in embarrassment. My neighbors must have heard every word.

A week later, a new island-style nightclub opened up behind Freddy's house. It wasn't air-conditioned, so huge speakers blasted 120-decibel bass lines through open windows until four in the morning. When Freddy came to work hoarse, I asked what happened.

He sheepishly replied, "I ran outside in my underwear last night and cussed out the disco."

I laughed and confessed what I'd done. The crazy dive instructors were out in force.

Freddy came into Tata's one night with his head in his hands.

"What's wrong this time?" I asked.

"I'm going crazy. I was listening to the chickens while I was falling asleep last night, and I could understand everything they were saying to each other."

I looked down at my rum and coke. "Yeah, I've had that happen to me, too."

After we were pretty hammered, I noticed Freddy's bleary eyes staring at me.

When I met his gaze, he said, "Bruk, Bruk, Bruk, Bruk-Bruk Bruk BraBruk."

Without hesitation, I answered, "Bruk, Bruk, Babruk, Bruk-Bruk."

After a few cock-a-doodle-doo-s, the conversation ended. Tata thought this was hilarious. Klaus looked at us like we were liquored-up idiots.

After a three-month probationary period, the resort asked me to commit to a full year contract. The answer was easy after I weighed the great diving and fantastic benefits against my backwoods lifestyle and gloating rooster nemesis. Two weeks later, I was on my way back to California.

After leaving the house for the last time, my next door neighbor stopped me to show off something that made her proud. Seven baby chicks were happily chirping in her courtyard. Dark streaks ran through their straw-colored down. I had a good hunch who the father was. My backpack was on, and my dive bag was on my shoulder.

I said, "That's wonderful," and broke into a run down the dusty road.

I may not have had the best time in Saint Lucia, but I did learn a lifelong rule from my experiences. Whether barbecued, fried, roasted, or stewed, EAT AS MUCH CHICKEN AS YOU POSSIBLY CAN.

Notes:

Someone sent me a newspaper article written by Roy Rivenburg, Los Angeles Times staff writer (May 6, 1997). The headline read: *Don't Look Now, But Chickens Are Taking Over The World . . .*

They've got a plant in the White House. They outnumber people 4 to 1. Total conquest can't be far behind. He went on to explain that chickens: were originally bred, not for food, but for ring matches. It has become their nature to fight . . . and procreate. A rooster can mate twenty to thirty times a day, and geneticists are, as we speak, injecting eggs with vaccines to design indestructible superbirds.

-Watch out.

I e-mailed Freddy recently. He refrained from any suicide attempts, left shortly after I did, and is doing fine as a dive gear technician in Florida. After reading the chapters on Saint Lucia, he had the following comments: "You left out the Kamikaze mosquitoes (I still bear the scars from them), the power outages when, like clockwork, the power station ran out of diesel fuel almost every Friday night (the disco had its own generator, you'll recall), and the town kids pooping on the hospital helipad."

Typical Polynesian Frangipani lei. Aitutaki, Cook Islands

Bula! A young Wayan says Good Morning. Fiji

Bures in Yalombi Village, Waya Island, Fiji

A typical pub in Queensland, Australia

154

Yam and procession approaching king's house,
Ponape, Micronesia

Bad day for the hogs at the Pohnpeiian funeral

Onlookers at the pig slaughter. Pohnpeiian funeral. Ponape

Chuukese kids posing on WWII Japanese anti-naval
artillery. Moen Island, Truk Lagoon

Cold water diving. Carmel, California

Home Sweet Home. *Arawa* moored in the Hole in the Wall, Ngargol Island, Palau.

Thai kathoy on the strip. (Yes, that's really a guy.)

Soi Bangla, Patong Beach, Phuket.
Typical outdoor Buddhist shrine in Thailand.

Not a bad place to work. Railay Bay, Krabi, Thailand

Tuk-tuk on Soi Bangla. Country-western bar is behind and upstairs. Patong Beach, Phuket, Thailand

Sunset over Gili Meno. The distant clouds are forming over the volcanoes of Bali. Gili Islands, Indonesia.

Recovering from my bizarre ankle condition at the dive shop. Supreme Headquarters, Gili Air, Indonesia

BACK TO PALAU

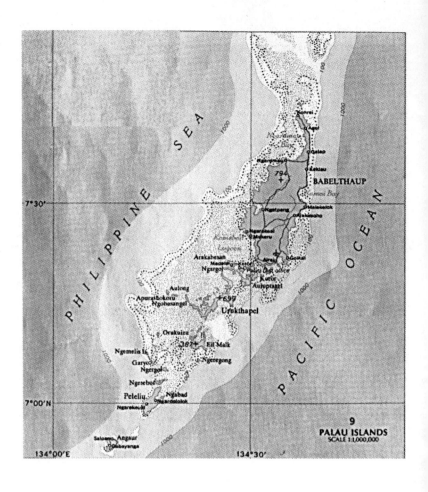

162

THE SACRAMENTO CONTINGENT
California

"Well, I guess you pick your poison." Barton

When I flew into San Francisco, Christine, my girlfriend from Palau, then a student at Cal State Sacramento, drove down to pick me up at the airport. After months of "I love you" telephone calls to me, I had taken the bait. I was back in the land of numbered streets and parking meters.

Many weeks later, on what would normally have been another beautiful Sunday morning, Monica called me out of the blue from Bermuda to tell me she was coming into town on business two days later. The *other* woman was under the covers with me when I picked up the phone. Unprepared, I couldn't think of anything to say that wouldn't let Christine know who was on the line.

Monica figured out what was going on in about two seconds and blew a blood vessel. "What do you mean you can't see me?" Pacific princess overheard the ensuing tirade and threw her own fit. "Why are you talking to the woman I stole you from?" There I was happily minding my own business one minute, and the next . . .

Hell hath no fury . . . ? Instead of talking about it, Monica sat home, letting the phone ring while she plunged Caribbean juju pins into my effigy. How do I get myself into these messes? Maybe from watching Mutiny on the Bounty too many times — all those topless Polynesian women had left a substantial imprint on me, and they all seemed to look like a certain Palauan.

Monica had been a best friend — smart, professional, fun, and unselfish — especially when it came to lassoing me. Don't forget rich and generous. My brown sugar mama. To me, she *was* Bermuda: predictable, affluent, polished, educated, and holding the promise of a happy future. I had given up that stability for an unpredictable destiny in a place nobody knew existed: exotic, wild, beautiful, and crazy. It didn't matter that Christine was a self-centered heartbreaker — a demon working the sex angle — a shark swimming in a medium of men. I had found passion.

ْ ‌

ৰ ৰ ৰ

A week later, in her bedroom, Christine is in one of her moods. Which of her five personalities is it this time? Loving housewife? Flamboyant playgirl? Devil incarnate? Devious home wrecker? Sex machine in overdrive? Apparently it's the last. Alone in the bedroom, Satan's little cabana-girl strips to her tiger-striped undies, turns, and places her hands flat on the wall in full primate display. Over her shoulder comes the inviting look practiced a thousand times in mirrors, and possibly on as many men.

The satin hits the floor as a vision clouds my sight. Transposed across the convex designs of her tailgate is a message. "If you can read this, you are too close." As always with her, I half-heartedly attempt to hit the brakes only to find that all the fluid has once again leaked out into the lower drive mechanism. What am I doing? I'm stuck in traffic, obsessed — rear ending a high mileage model with a warning from the Surgeon General tattooed on her fender.

ৰ ৰ ৰ

Six months later, I am once again at *Chez Christine*, a shabby house off Twelfth Street where all the displaced Palauan students are shacked up together. Few Americans visit the house because the Palauans prefer to hang out with their own.

Watching TV is the preferred activity. Jeopardy comes on at 7:30, and then it's time for a new batch of kung fu rental videos. The brown eyes focused on the screen impart a silent message.

"We're lonely. We don't belong here. Take us home to our islands."

The youngest brother is eating dinner from a plate on the floor. He has been in the States for only three days and can't deal with dinner tables yet. The entree is duck.

That started me wondering. "Where did you guys get the duck? Chinatown?"

"At the park with our slingshots."

"You mean the state park where the American River joins the Sacramento?"

"Yeah, that one."

"Oh."

You can take the boys out of the islands, but . . .

Paradise called — her home — my dreamland. After eleven months, it was time to return to the lesser latitudes. She dropped out of school. I went through the familiar cycle of quitting my job, selling my car, and storing my stuff. Could I escape the wrath of every Caribbean voodoo entity on the opposite side of the globe? Only one way to find out.

Goodbye, cold November rain.

PALAUAN MAGIC
Palau

"The universe is full of magical things patiently waiting for our wits to grow sharper." Eden

"Formerly, when religion was strong and science weak, men mistook magic for medicine, now, when science is strong and religion weak, men mistake medicine for magic." Thomas

Marfa, Texas, is famous for having displays of glowing balls over the desert floor on calm nights. A friend of mine said he saw a ball like this inexplicably following railroad tracks on a summer night in North Carolina. He was on the tracks at the time and ducked as it went past. These apparitions are probably related to St. Elmo's Fire, a glowing ball of static electricity sometimes seen at night on ships' mastheads.

Other than natural phenomena, proper magic exists in Palau also. Sorcery was prominent in the culture, and despite modern times, a few people still possess powers. Palauans are very superstitious. Bizarre love matches (like mine) are often attributed to black magic in local rumors.

I discovered that Palau had special energies while sleeping on secluded Ulong beach. I felt the wind blow through me, kindling my spirit, and boosting the power in my soul — magically soothing. I have been in few places as spiritual.

The Palauans are respectful of the energies of some of the islands. Some are not to be visited at all. Every now and then, someone ignores the taboo, like the couple who went ashore on a sacred island to harvest coconuts a few years ago. Shortly after crossing the beach, coconuts began flying

at them from the treetops, thwarting their attempt and chasing them back to their boat.

The stars hung motionless in the inky black sky as our boat tore across the dark water at forty knots. Running unlit, Christine's Uncle Gil used the dim silhouettes of surrounding islands to navigate through the intricate pattern of shallow reefs in the lagoon. Hitting one at that speed would be fatal, but I wasn't worried. He had been cruising those waters for almost fifty years.

I was spending Thanksgiving with Christine and her relatives. They lived in a cove in the rock islands and did nothing but fish for a living. I had been invited along on the trip that night.

Our vessel was a typical Palauan boat, 32 feet long, open-hulled fiberglass, and powered by twin 200-horsepower outboard engines. The forward half of the boat was heaped full with nets. A beautiful green V of phosphorescence from bioluminescent plankton fanned out behind the propellers. The bow wave also glowed in the dark, as well as the spray flying to the side. Lying on the bow, I noticed five-foot diameter glowing balls, about twenty feet deep, lighting up in the water in front of the boat. How could the plankton be stimulated if it was ahead of us? I asked the cousin next to me what was causing it.

He shrugged and mumbled, "Magic."

That prompted me to ask him about other strange phenomena that I'd heard about. Sometimes, on dead calm nights, silent glowing balls wander over the lagoon. They have been described as being five to ten feet in diameter, and five to thirty feet high in the air. When I mentioned it, he nodded yes, he had seen it. When I asked what caused it, he shrugged again.

"How many times have you seen it?"

"Many times."

"From how close?"

"Very close at Peleliu. Maybe fifty feet. One came across the lagoon very slowly and went into the top of a coconut palm like a chicken and stayed there for a few minutes, then went away."

After lining up distant landmarks in three directions, Gil throttled back the engines, shut them off, and raised them so they wouldn't bang on the reef as the tide went out. It was still a few hours before sunrise, so we dropped anchor and got as comfortable as possible on the hard deck for some sleep.

At first light, the normally lackadaisical family members were full of energy. Our objective was to catch *um* (pronounced like boom), the fattest and tastiest of the unicorn fish — a Palauan delicacy. *Um* only cross the reef once a month, so we had to be ready for that rendezvous. The location was a family secret and I was sworn to silence.

We hopped into knee deep water, and with Gil in command, rolled out over a thousand feet of five-foot wide net to form a huge V on the edge of the barrier reef. The opening faced out to sea, and a net cage was in the rear corner. There were a dozen of us, and everybody was assigned a specific job. Mine was to help chase the fish into the corner when they showed up.

I wondered how many centuries this family had been netting *um* there by the light of the rising sun. Did they even know? I had stumbled onto an innate part of their heritage.

When the tide changed just after sunrise, we got into our ready positions at the ends of the V and waited in silence. Gil squatted in the middle with a mask and snorkel. There was a minor crisis when a reef shark swam into the catch area so we all rushed after it, slapping the surface with our hands to chase it away. Then we hurried back into position. The waiting was tense.

Water flew high as Gil leapt up, ripped out his snorkel, and started screaming commands in Palauan. The fish were coming across the reef. Scrambling fast under a deluge of orders that spared no niceties, we closed the V with a long string of plastic streamers carried between us. As we rushed the back corner, the school of panicky fish packed into a dark cloud of thrashing muscle between our shins and the net cage. We slowly moved forward, crouching, with our hands in the water, crowding them in. Gil was screaming at us to stay together. If a few fish discovered an escape hole, the rest would follow. Not until the cage was drawn shut did everyone relax. Hauling the writhing catch to the boat wasn't nearly as difficult as lifting it out of the water. When the last flapping fish was piled in the boat, we re-stacked the nets on the bulwarks and climbed aboard.

The job was finished, so everyone sprawled out, dropping back into their normal state of relaxation as the pile twitched its final throes. Gil's wife pulled out a lime, knife, and soy sauce, and began to cut strips of sashimi for us. The fresh meat quivered slightly as the filet knife stripped it away.

It was time to sell the catch. I estimated over a thousand pounds of fish aboard and was amazed at the family's talent when I saw that every fish was an um. (Normally nets pull in all kinds of fish.) We went up to Koror, the nation's center, and docked next to the fish market. When we got there, the young men pulled out a couple hundred pounds to bestow on their dozens of relatives as a Thanksgiving present. The rest sold at $2.50 a pound, which was enough to cover the family finances for a couple of weeks or more. Watching wads of cash trading hands drove home the importance of the venture and explained why Gil was screaming so much at us during the catch.

After fueling the boat, we returned to their home in the rock islands. I enjoyed a new form of Palauan magic as we cooked up our own version of the holiday with a wonderful Fishgiving feast.

WELCOME TO THE FIFTH WORLD
Palau

"You can't be a real country unless you have a beer and an airline. It helps if you have some kind of football team or some nuclear weapons, but at the very least, you need a beer." Zappa

"It is always difficult, even dangerous, to return to a world that has transported you, and epiphanies rarely repeat themselves." Pico

Because of the sea's massive food resources and abundance of fruitful land, no one has ever starved in Palau. The country is not impoverished, so I don't consider it a developing country (unless the new billiards hall counts). It's in its own category — not the third world. It's way beyond anything we're familiar with. It's not even the fourth world. It's the fifth world.

After two-and-a-half years of telling everyone, including myself, that I would return to Palau, I did. I arrived full of prospective business ideas now that the territory had become an independent nation. However, the Palauan government had conveniently overlooked the clause in the Compact of Free Association with the United States concerning the privilege for Americans to work freely in the country. To top off my disappointment, my predictably doomed relationship with my girlfriend ended a week later. I didn't even have a place to live because my old boat, the *Hose Queen*, had sunk. At least, I had good diving to look forward to, but, as they say . . . you can never go back.

December 22, 1994

Greetings from a small town community, a place where it is impossible to go anywhere without running into someone who knows you. Sound travels faster than light, especially for a big blonde target like me. Everyone always seems to know what I had for lunch, where I've been, and who I've been with, so I feel compelled to be on my best behavior. It's a big change from my native Los Angeles, and because of that, I have adapted a new social skill — learning how to get along with *everyone*. In the city, I can tell some jerk where to go and never need to see them again. Here, I see everyone, all the time.

Palauans rarely talk, which makes them seem aloof to outsiders. When someone walks into a house, they don't say, "Hi, nice to see you. How have you been?" They sit silently, entrenched in their personal domain. I took it personally until I realized that they didn't greet each other, either. This is hard on divers who expect briefings from the local divemasters. "Blue Corner, forty minutes," is not satisfactory for customers who are used to twenty-minute chalkboard discussions.

Raising the eyebrows for affirmation is a normal conversation technique in Palau. (This subtle gesture is common across the Pacific and works in Southeast Asia as well). When I first arrived, a Palauan charter captain I'd never met picked up my divers from the dock. I hadn't heard a sound from his lips all morning, so after anchoring the boat at the Blue Holes, I sidled up next to him to make sure he knew what to do. The current was strong, and if he didn't pick us up, we'd end up in New Guinea.

I motioned toward the open sea. "After we exit the grotto, we're going to drift in that direction. You should be able to follow our bubbles. Can you pick us up over there in 45 minutes or so?"

He raised his eyebrows together and let them drop.

I didn't know if he'd ever picked up divers before, or if he could even speak English. I repeated my instructions and asked if he understood.

He raised his eyebrows again very slowly.

I took that to mean, "I heard you the first time," so I stopped worrying and went diving. When we surfaced, the boat waiting a few yards away from us. The relaxed driver was slouched in the captain's chair with his feet up under the console. He was preparing a chew of betel nut for himself and didn't bother to glance over at us. He was obviously a seasoned dive boat captain. I never did hear him speak.

Palau has a unique cultural hierarchy that is interesting for many reasons. One is that women make the most important traditional decisions, such as who will be the next chief. Another is that powerful high caste elders, including the chiefs, can more or less rule this modern country in traditional fashion, despite the decisions or protests of the elected democratic government.

A classic example is the story of the high chief's curfew of 1992. After a dispute with some local teenagers, the chief became incensed at their lack of respect. In the past, a chief could have had them and their families put to death. This seemed a little drastic for the nineties, so he imposed a nightly ten-o'clock curfew over his realm, the state of Koror. The police enforced this, so the level of night life in town plunged overnight to less than that of an Iowa suburb.

The bar and nightclub owners were hard hit by the decree. One, a lesser chief from the southernmost island state of Peleliu, decided to keep his doors open after ten in protest. He was summarily banned for an indefinite period from Koror, and exiled back to his native coconut patch. As of this writing, the ban is still in effect. He is still cooling his heels down there, unforgiven. This is like being banished from New York City to Des Moines — and it's not like he can sneak back for a little action. Remember the jungle network.

Cars here are driven until they die. Old veterans are held together with tape, grime, and what's left of their paint job. Rust marks perforate fenders, mufflers drag, and hub caps have bounced into roadside ditches. A few don't have windows. Some are left-hand drive from the States. Others have the steering wheel on the right, Japanese style. One tourist wondered which side of the road they should be on as his taxi driver careened down the middle of the potholed road from the airport.

He asked, "Which side do you drive on here? Left or right?"

The driver, thinking he was referring to the steering wheel placement, said, "It doesn't matter."

The tourist, sensing an imminent head-on, yelled, "It certainly does matter!"

𐁮 𐁮 𐁮

After the war, the United Nations appointed the United States caretakers of the region. The US mission was to develop agriculture and industry in the new territory. Instead, the many millions of dollars from US aid went indirectly into personal comforts, such as new Toyota trucks and 400-horsepower boats. I can't help thinking, "Why do these guys have brand new 20,000 dollar boats and trucks and I don't?" The American diplomats must have thought they were going to get something in return for all this money. Nope. When it comes to "What can you do for me?" attitudes, Palauans are the champs. They can roam into our country whenever they please, live there, receive scholarships from our universities, and own land. Americans, however, still have to pay fifty dollars a month for visa extensions in Palau, can't own land, can't start a business without paying a 10,000 dollar fee, and can't work without hard-to-obtain permits.

A typical example of this attitude is the story of Palau's government power plant. When bidding was opened for the contract, a large British construction company flew the Palauan chiefs and politicians to Paris and London where they were wined and dined as an incentive to accept the astronomically

174

high offer. They were also given six digit checks. This was supposed to be very "hush-hush," of course. The contract was signed, the plant was built, but a nosy American organization called the FBI figured out what was going on.

Copies of the canceled bribe checks, including the endorsing signatures on the backs were published in the newspaper. Scandal hits Palau! So what? The signatures were those of prominent businessmen and chiefs who were also related to a significant portion of the population. At the thought of actually prosecuting these guys, most Palauans laughed until they rolled off their lanais in hysterics. Partially chewed betel nut fell wasted to the ground. "Tell us something we don't know . . . ha ha ha, stop, stop, it hurts. Don't make us laugh so hard. Stop." Nothing happened of course. The "debauched" leaders and businessmen are doing well and are still prominent public figures.

Island logic prevailed. "If it was a shady deal, then we aren't going to pay." The bank is still trying to recover its loan from the country. Good luck.

෨෨ ෨෨ ෨෨

Despite the government putting monetary squeezes and restrictions on me as a foreigner, I feel freer than I did at home. Consider freedom as an absolute when it is partially defined: "exemption from external control, interference, regulation . . . " California is a police state by comparison.

American laws are created daily and have grown so numerous that they effect every aspect of our lives. For example, nobody has the skill to drive across town without committing at least one violation. New laws are accepted in lieu of effectively confronting an issue, and the process has become a stampede of waste, unable to be stopped by any single cowboy.

It's easy at home to get a parking ticket if a car tire is over a painted line, but they don't have painted lines here, or parking meters, or police helicopters for that matter. As long as I don't upset anyone, I can do anything I want anywhere in the country.

I can launch a boat without the Coast Guard watching, drink beer in public, have a fire on the beach, and do it all while carrying both volumes of Palauan law around in one hand. To top things off, the cops don't hassle people. Sure, they make arrests when needed, but they are <u>nice</u>.

So here I am thinking of what I'm missing at home: high taxes, crime, pollution, bankrupt school districts, poverty, homelessness . . . maybe it's better to ignore that and stay focused on the easy life here. In fact, now would be a good time to go fishing in my secret cove. There, beneath the limestone cliffs, I can anchor in the shade and watch the frigate birds and cockatoos flapping peacefully from tree to tree. The only sounds will be their calls, and the water lapping against the hull. One thing I won't need to do first is buy a fishing license.

MANTA FEVER
Palau

"Why is your job so much like my vacation?" question from a customer on McCready's boat

June 11, 1995

It's sunset, and our sailboat is moored outside of German Channel. McCready has just started the coals for the twenty-pound mackerel we caught today. The drinks have been poured, and everybody is relaxed and happy after a great day's diving. There's not much wind and the water is reflecting red and orange hues from the clouds in the west. There are a few ripples in the water thirty feet behind the boat, and what appears to be dolphin or shark fins at first, turns out to be three manta rays holding their right wing tips up as they languidly turn. They are making feeding passes back and forth across the channel, and do a dozen more circuits as the sun sets. Palauan magic again.

Less than a hundred yards away, sixty feet deep, is a low outcrop where mantas regularly come by to be cleaned by wrasse. Divers sit around in the sand just uphill from the stone as if it were an amphitheater stage. If they are lucky, they may see up to a dozen of these giant rays during one dive. The mantas pull up to the rock, open their gills and mouths, and let the little wrasse go to work. Some of them are twenty-five feet across, casting dark shadows over entire groups of divers as they pass. As long as the divers hold still and don't make a fence around the area with their bubbles, the mysterious giants keep coming back.

During our last dive today, we sat for thirty uneventful minutes at the cleaning station. It was a rare strikeout, so I led the divers a hundred yards to a lively shark spot. A couple of black tips were swimming around, and the bigger fish were chasing schools of one-inch fry, picking stragglers off for dinner. One school scattered away from a trevally and regrouped above me. The rays of the late-afternoon sun were filtered into flickering beams by the cloud of fish, creating an ethereal fantasy scene in the slightly murky water. Then they suddenly shot directly down towards me. Thousands of fish parted inches away from my mask before darting around my head. After the last fish passed, I saw what had frightened them. Backlit by the sun, a huge spade-shaped silhouette soared slowly.

Another manta form emerged out of the sunlight. Flapping gracefully, they glided right over us. I looked back and saw two more coming . . .

then another shape emerged . . .

and another . . .

and another.

Seven mantas were winging lazy circles in the water overhead.

KEVIN AND SARAH
Philippines/Palau

"Just think. The other kids are in school right now." Kevin, enjoying his vacation in the Philippines

Kevin, from Arkansas, worked with me in Palau. When we blew into the Philippines on a visa run, we headed straight for Puerto Galera on the island of Mindoro, where a cabana beach known for diving (and go-go bars) awaited us.

The best thing about the dive sites on Mindoro is the tremendous color diversity in the abundant crinoids. Also known as feather stars or sea lilies, these echinoderms (related to starfish, sea urchins, and sand dollars) are some of my favorite underwater critters. One of the most advanced invertebrates, these animals crawl around on numerous spindly legs to get to ideal feeding grounds. Once located on top of a coral head or perched on the end of a wire coral, they use more than two-dozen fern-like "arms" to gather plankton, often flattening their normal rosebud shape into two parallel fans that are aligned at right angles to the current for maximum catching ability. To swim, they alternately wave their "arms" in a rhythmic, merry-go-round style cycle. If they fall and land upside down, they can turn upright in seconds. When not feeding, they curl up into pincushion-like balls.

As a geologist, I have been a fan of crinoids ever since I found a limestone bed full of fossil crinoid stems in the back of a Colorado cave, 12,000 feet above sea level. The skeletons indicated that the ancient animals were at least ten times larger than their modern descendants.

After our day of diving, we headed up to the strip to check out the discos. Kevin ended up with a buxom Filipina bar girl who claimed she was eighteen, but looked more like sixteen.

After a few days of staying with her, he found out that she was actually fifteen, which explained why she wanted candy while we were drinking Red Horse Ale. The next day over coffee, Kevin told me that she had confessed to actually being thirteen. I figured that was his problem. The morning after that, he looked glum.

"Mike?"

"Yeah?"

"She's twelve" (pronounced tway-elve in Arkansian).

"What?"

"I'd marry her except that she's not old enough, so I thought I could adopt her."

"Kevin, that would be really funny if you weren't serious."

"No, listen. I've got it worked out. If I adopt her, I can claim her as a dependent on my taxes and deduct 3,500 dollars a year. I figured I'd just give her whatever money I saved to keep her out of the bars."

"That's very noble, but I think you'd better quit while you're still not in prison."

He ended up sending her back to her hometown with a hundred bucks. Unfortunately, it was probably her parents who sent her to the bars originally. Life can be rough out there.

When Kevin and I got back from the Philippines, we fell right back into our routine of sitting around after work and drinking beer with the other staff at the dive shop. Like the Palauans, we chewed betel nut, particularly when its effects were amplified by alcohol.

A betel nut "chew" is prepared by cracking a nut apart, mixing one half with lime, and wrapping it in pepper leaf. It is then placed between the cheek and gum, turning saliva temporarily red and producing a mild effect similar to chewing tobacco. Hard-core chewers end up with permanent crimson stains in their mouths. When they get old, people who started chewing as kids acquire blackened gums and eventually lose their teeth. Public ground space in Palau is splotched red from spitting.

180

Instead of having a proper "boo" bag for his nuts, leaf, and lime, Kevin carried his fixings around in a cardboard Marlboro carton. One night, we were sitting around the dive shop when a boat pulled up to the dock. A haole woman I'd never met before got off.

Kevin moaned, "Oh, no. It's Sarah."

"Who's that?"

"A new school teacher. Came a few weeks ago and is a major pain in the butt."

She came up, pleasantly introduced herself to me, sat down, and stubbed her cigarette out in Kevin's Marlboro box, thinking it was trash. I saw his ears redden as he fumed silently.

When Sarah said she wanted to go diving with us the next day, Kevin shot me a warning look. Thinking I could handle whatever I was getting into, I ignored it and welcomed her to join us.

She showed up on time for the morning dive, and off we went. Yellow Wall started where an estuary drained into the sea from the island of Peleliu. Because of the brackish layer of lagoon sludge floating on the saltwater, the top of the wall, only thirty feet deep, was hidden from us on the boat. It was tricky to judge where to start. Everyone could mistakenly end up on top of the reef if we went in at the wrong place or didn't descend fast enough in the current. If that happened, we would have to do a long swim to get back over the lip of the reef, missing the best part of the wall. It was my responsibility to make sure we hit it right.

As we approached the lagoon entrance, I asked everybody to get ready and went up to the bow to check the current. Sarah put on her weight belt, and on what normally would have been another beautiful day, fell overboard. She didn't come back up. I grabbed my mask and screamed at people to get out of the way as I ran down the boat. I couldn't see her through the cloudy water, but had to get her before she drowned.

Just before I dove, her head popped up ten yards astern. I hit the brakes, relieved. Then she sunk again and I was back in emergency mode. I sprung out as far as I could with my mask in

181

hand, and put it on as I swam down to her. When I cleared it, I saw her struggling wildly to get back to the surface. I grabbed her weightbelt and hauled her up. At the surface, I pulled the quick release buckle and tossed the free belt over my shoulder. She was out of breath, but okay. She tried acting nonchalant in front of everyone else, but I knew how close she had come.

Next time, I'll pay attention to warnings from Kevin.

THE LEGEND OF MAD BEN OF AIRAI
Palau

"His mouth was writing checks his body couldn't cash."
Darrell, Tyrant of the Palau Hash

Palauan legends are preserved on ornately engraved mahogany storyboards. The characters are depicted in several scenes representing the key events, and each board is labeled with the name of the tale. Prisoners hand carve the majority of the boards because they have nothing better to do in jail. They peddle their products to visiting tourists for 25 to 500 dollars a board, depending on its size.

Ben was an American guy who lived in Airai, a village on the nearby island of Babelthaup. He often hung around the dive shop during the evening social hours, bothering people with bullshit stories – an obnoxious habit that got exponentially worse when he drank. One Saturday, he joined us for the bimonthly hash run (nothing to do with hashish) on an evening that would be heard about in the farthest reaches of the nation.

The hash is best described as "a drinking club with a running problem." After its formation by expatriates in Malaysia in 1938, its popularity spread worldwide. There are now hash runs in almost every country. In Palau we did live hashes, that is, two or three "hares" led the pack of "hounds" on a wild chase through the jungle to a secret location. After a ten-minute head start, the hares dropped flour on the trail to mark it. Dirty tricks such as making more than one trail were common. If the hounds caught the hares, or better yet, figured out where they are going and beat them there, they got their shorts. Coolers stuffed with ice and beer waited at the on-home finish. After sunset, a bonfire was lit, and *religion* took place – an esoteric series of strange rituals, each concluded by a *down-down* (draining twelve ounces

183

of beer from the sacred vessel at once). Sport drinking follows the formalities and continues until the coolers are empty. When the festivities conclude, the fire is extinguished in exotic fashion, adjourning the meeting for two weeks.

The original founders of the Palau hash are a group of expats who have lived there for ten to twenty-five years. Most have Palauan families, and all speak the language fluently. The hash is a fixture in their lives. On Ben's first run, he was obligated to chug a *down-down* by the fire and introduce himself. One of the questions somebody asked him was why he hadn't come to a hash before.

Already drunk, he said, "Because I hang out with my Palauan friends, not like you idiots who just hang out with each other."

After making an ass out of himself, he grabbed a beer, and came over to stand next to me.

"What did you say *that* for?" I asked. (Rule number 22 dash C: never antagonize a drunk.)

Our conversation regressed to mutual insults and Ben got it into his head that we had to fight. He always boasted that he was a trained killer, and able to butcher someone in a few seconds. I never believed him, and since I was bigger, I stayed where I was, leaning against a pickup truck. I tried to ignore him, but he moved around in front of me, pressing the challenge.

"Fuck you, Mike. I'm going to kick your ass right here, right now."

He repeated himself until I snapped, jumped forward, and gave him a pair of black eyes. Getting hit only made him madder, and he continued to shout threats for the next hour while a couple of guys held him away in the shadows. It was the first fight in the history of the Palau hash — definitely not appropriate behavior. A lot of people were pissed off.

After the hash, I went home, showered, and was lounging around watching TV when there was a knock on the door. I opened it, and there stood Ben.

"Hey Ben. What's up?"

"Oh, so you won't fight me," he muttered as he came charging into the dark living room, swinging what looked like a club at my head.

I reacted quickly, stepping forward to block the blow with my left arm while pounding my best right into his nose. He flew back through the front doorway and landed on his back on the concrete porch. The momentum of the punch caused me to land on top of him. He tried to get up, so I smacked his head into the floor and felt his body go limp. A crimson pool spread rapidly from under his head. Blood spurted up out of his nose and mouth. I thought I'd killed him, but he had a pulse. I called an ambulance.

The landlord, who lived next door, walked up with a flashlight.

"What the hell's going on, here?"

Ben was still out cold across the threshold of the front door.

"This guy tried to hit me with a club, so I punched him."

He gestured at the lawn near Ben's outstretched arms. "Uh . . . that's not a club, my friend."

The flashlight beam rested on a machete.

When I saw it, I was mad enough to hit him again, but the police were arriving along with the ambulance. Ben went to intensive care, and I went downtown in bracelets. After I wrote out a statement claiming self-defense, the cops drove me home.

The next morning, I went down to the Rock Island Café for a cup of coffee and a greasy American breakfast. I joined my friend Hank and related my story while he listened in stunned silence. Afterward, we went across the street to Drew's house and told him what happened. Hank used the phone to call the hospital to inquire about Ben's condition. After a few minutes of listening to a nurse, he said thank you, left our number, and hung up.

"Well?"

"They said he might die. He's in critical condition."

"Holy shit."

When I realized that I might become a murderer, I went into a state of shock. Time crawled as we sat waiting for the phone to ring. Drew was one of the government attorneys and began laying out the legal picture for me. After an hour, Hank couldn't stand the tension and called the nurse back. Ben had regained consciousness and was no longer in danger of dying. We relaxed, relieved, as Drew brewed another pot of coffee. Hank decided to pay Ben a visit and left for the hospital.

Although Ben's entire head was wrapped in gauze with tubes stuck in his nose, he was talkative as ever. Because he was a few years older than I was, he told Hank, "I can't believe I got my ass kicked by a kid."

"Mike's a pretty big kid, don't forget."

"Tell him I still want to fight."

"You might want to wait until you're looking better."

"How do I look?"

"You ain't no oil painting."

Ben had a dozen stitches in the back of his head, a concussion, and a broken nose. He was blind in one eye for three days, and in the other, three weeks.

Hank met us afterward at the dive shop and gave us the update. As I repeated the story to everyone who walked in, Hank sketched a mock storyboard on the briefing chalkboard, depicting the night's events with a twist of humor. Everyone liked it, so he took up a collection and went to see the carvers at the prison.

I was one of the hares for the next hash, Run #222, a.k.a. sadistic-jungle-thrash-from-hell. When planning the route, we looked at photos in a book taken from wartime fighter planes and saw what looked like an old road running across the top of a steep-sided island. This was supposed to be our clever shortcut, but it turned out that it was only a clearing for a power line. The hash run ended up as a knee-bashing epic over sharp limestone boulders.

Everyone survived, and we had the fire on a high hill overlooking the harbor and rock islands. Ben didn't show up, which was good because The Legend of Mad Ben of Airai was unveiled at Religion. It was an 18 by 24-inch mahogany board depicting all of the night's events. I was shown in a loincloth with my hair in a Palauan topknot, as was Ben. My apartment became a traditional thatch meeting house. Re-bar stuck out of the grass roof to imitate Filipino laborers' habit of leaving support for an upper floor if the lower one stands for awhile without collapsing. The landlord bellowed fire. Other scenes showed handcuffs and hospital beds. Cries of "On-On!" came from the runners on the hills in the background. Ben stood next to a fire chugging a *down-down* with a Pinocchio-style donkey tail hanging from his backside. It was perfect for its purpose.

I was called to center stage to do several *down-downs* as penance. When I finished, I apologized to everyone for my actions at the previous hash and thanked them for having a sense of humor about the whole situation.

That's not what they wanted to hear.

Someone yelled out, "We want to know how hard you hit him."

"As hard as I could."

A cheer went up from the crowd of barbarians. I didn't expect that. The R.A. (our leader) came forward and officially changed my hash name to Iron Mike.

The storyboard is currently on display at the dive shop.

THE BATTLE FOR PELELIU
Palau

"When we hit the beach, I went over the side. It was a long jump . . . like falling into hell. The beach was being hit by heavy small-arms fire and mortars and artillery. There were bodies and parts of bodies all around. I was terrified."

"That night the Japs hit us in the dark, and it created a hell of a mess. I patched up the wounded by feeling my hands for blood, because many of the men didn't know where they were hit."

"Along the shore, Jap dead washed in with the tide and bled on the sand . . . In the countless gullies and basins, the Jap dead lay four deep, and on the level stretches they were scattered in one layer . . . sprawled in ghastly attitudes . . . "

"Many were huddled with their arms around each other as though they had futilely tried to protect themselves from our fire . . . horribly mutilated, riddled by bullets and torn by shrapnel."

"I don't think anyone really knew how bad things were until the fifth day, when we were brought off the lines into reserve. We hadn't eaten except for the C-rations we had in our packs. I remember some Navy guys carrying large containers of hot chow finally located us. A chief petty officer said he had food for fifty men and asked, 'where the hell are the rest of your guys?' It was then we looked around and counted . . . there were eighteen of us left." from 1 Marine division survivors of Peleliu

" . . . I told you that one of these days we'd get the shit shot out of us during a landing." Colonel Chesty Puller, commander of the 1st Marine regiment, commenting at the beachhead on the first day to First Lieutenant Frank Sheppard

Today, Peleliu is a peaceful island with two small villages, 500 inhabitants, coral roads, and lush jungle. The local pastimes are fishing, drinking Budweiser, and cultivating high-grade marijuana. What most people don't know is that it was one of the bloodiest battlegrounds of the Pacific war. For almost three months in the autumn of 1944, this serene island was a blazing hell. The 13,000 Japanese soldiers that were posted here had over a year to fortify against the impending American attack. Without any hope of withstanding the forthcoming assault, their mission was to inflict as much damage to the enemy as possible. Their orders were "don't surrender." They didn't.

Many US Marine and Navy commanders knew the island could be bypassed. However, politics led them to continue with the invasion. The Navy commenced the attack by pounding the Japanese for two days with 2500 artillery rounds and 1800 bombs dropped from aircraft. After surveying the smoldering shore, naval commanders halted their bombardment a day early because "there were no more targets." Marine commanders boasted that the island would be captured in three days or less. Two months later, they were still mired in their fiasco. The blunder of committing to the invasion slowed the war campaign and caused over 20,000 American and Japanese young men to be killed or badly wounded – one for every third word in this book.

When the marines crossed the reef on the morning of September 15, they were cut down on the western beaches in a vicious crossfire from ground level bunkers. Cannon and mortar shells blew bodies to pieces. The sea and sand were red from the blood. As darkness fell, only fifty yards of ground had been gained in the area of the heaviest fighting. An epic bayonet fight around midnight saved the one area of high ground. If it had been lost, the pinned marines would have been driven back into the ocean the next morning.

After three days of non-stop combat, the Japanese were forced back to the fortified caves of the limestone ridges on the west coast of the island. They had nothing left to do but kill as many invaders as possible and wait for their own ugly deaths. As the fight raged on, every living thing around the ridges was reduced to ashes. From the white cliffs towering over the blackened moonscape, Japanese machine-gunners could set up a crossfire deathtrap against any who dared approach. There was no natural cover left, so attempts to advance on the high ground resulted in slaughter.

Some battalions sustained casualties over 70 percent and were withdrawn − the first battle in history where the US Marines couldn't finish a fight. Almost half of the troops that went ashore on the first day left the island on stretchers, badly wounded or dead. They were replaced by the Army's 81 Infantry Division, who had already taken the nearby island of Angaur. After months of dogged assaults, the Americans finally controlled the ridge tops. They killed the last resisters by pouring fuel down into the caves and lighting it.

The official end came when the Japanese commander committed hara-kiri atop Bloody Nose Ridge. The only Japanese left alive out of 13,000 were a couple hundred Okinawan laborers and two-dozen undiscovered troops who hung on until 1947 before surrendering.

Divers have lunchtime picnics now at the end of the invasion beach and often set up tours of the battlefields with one of the local van owners. Tanks lie rusting where they were hit; Zeroes lie in the undergrowth; artillery pieces point seaward from their caves, and live ordnance occupies old boxes on the ground. There are still Japanese bones in some of the more remote caves. I don't think I'll ever be able to sit on Bloody Beach and not get a lump in my throat when I think about the massacre.

JAWS
Palau

"Its head shook violently from side to side, and its body trembled, snakelike. A piece of flesh tore away . . . Soon another shark appeared, and another, and the water began to roil."
Peter

The current is ripping hard on Blue Corner, a vertical wedge jutting into the flow of the Philippine Sea from Palau's barrier reef. I am holding on to the top edge of the reef, facing into the current. Gray reef sharks are gliding all around. A five-footer drifts casually into place two feet away. Its tail languidly sweeps back and forth in front of my face. A mischievous impulse dares me to touch the caudal appendage, but I'm worried about the owner snapping around to bite like a Doberman. Curiosity and excitement build as my decision is made. Reaching out hesitantly, I gently brush a fingertip against the rasp-like skin. The shark's only reaction is to move up, just out of reach.

In mating season, sharks circle in schools of fifty or more, their skins torn by the teeth of males. Females are bitten during mating, and males lose flesh in fights for dominance. I once witnessed a male suddenly turn and bite a nearby rival, puncturing a foot-wide eye-shaped perforation into his hide. I muttered OUCH into my regulator.

Despite a ferocious reputation, sharks drift docilely most of the time. Then, a silent signal is transmitted, and they simultaneously dart out of sight. Before, I wondered where they went. Now, I know.

On the lip of Blue Corner, a school of gray snapper next to me suddenly became wild-eyed and nervous, like a frantic flock trying to get away from a sheep dog. In the next instant, all the fish scattered and disappeared. Jaws cracked below me. I looked down to see two gray reef sharks ripping away at a large already-unrecognizable carcass. A third shark scared the hell out of me as it shot over my shoulder from behind to join them. I looked back to see a dozen more coming at me. I ducked as they rushed by and then watched them search for leftovers, impressed and exalted by their power. Fortunately, their small brains only recognize fish shapes as food. If they ever figure out that the outline of a scuba diver is easy pickings, we'll be the lunch.

Once at Peleliu, I looked up to see a huge school of parrotfish hurrying along the top of the wall. To the inside, between the fish and the island, were four huge tuna. Outside, three gray reef sharks helped the other big fish herd their prey. As they passed, the predators launched simultaneously into the school. Their snapping jaws sounded like wooden tables being whipped with wide leather belts. I felt a whooshing vibration of panicked acceleration as the parrotfish bolted for the safety of the depths. A half-second after the attack, no fish of any type lingered in sight. All that was left looked like snow falling. I swam over to find fish scales slowly sinking.

WHERE WAS HEMINGWAY?

Palau

"I could see the curve in the line and the next time he jumped he was astern and headed out to sea. Then he came out again and smashed the water white and I could see he was hooked in the side of his mouth. The stripes showed clear on him. He was a fine fish bright silver now, barred with purple, and a big around as a log." Papa

One morning, three of my friends came trooping down the dock for their weekly fishing trip. This time, however, they had a pair of long bamboo poles with them.

"What are those for?"

"They're outriggers for marlin. Why don't you come along and see for yourself?"

Hearing that they were after the mightiest of game fish inspired me to drop what I was doing and go. I had seen a million photos of these massive trophy fish hanging by their tails over docks. It was time to find out what the excitement was all about.

Jeff, an aircraft mechanic from Florida, was an experienced marlin fisherman and director of operations for the day. Dorji, a lawyer, hadn't done much more fishing than I had. Sam ran the dive shop and owned the boat. I was assigned the task of odd jobs and appointed O.B.O. (Official Beer Opener).

After a ten-mile cruise into open ocean, we deployed the gear. Deep-sea rods as thick as pool cues were slipped into holders. The two bamboo outriggers held extra lines to each side of the boat, making room for two more astern. Jeff produced a few mackerel from a cooler that still had some life left in them. He inserted large hooks down their throats before sewing their mouths shut on the steel leaders. The fish stayed alive under water, offering the ultimate lure.

Several hours of uneventful trolling later, I was starting to wonder if there were any marlin at all. I broke the first round of brewskies out of the ice chest and passed them around. Sam sipped and motored. Jeff cradled his bottle and sat in the rear watching the lines. On the foredeck, Dorji and I were sprawled on our backs in the sun, clumsily pouring beer into our mouths.

Suddenly, one of the reels whirred. Jeff snatched the rod and clipped it into a chest harness, shouting orders as the line darted back and forth in the water. Dorji and I jumped up to get the free lines in before they got tangled. Sam maneuvered the boat skillfully, trying not to pull too hard or let any slack build up in the line. Seconds later, the water erupted a hundred yards astern as a writhing ten foot marlin walked on its tail for a few seconds. Its shiny blue skin glinted beautifully in the sun as it tossed its head back and forth. Then the hook flew thirty feet in the air and the fish was gone. We drifted for a moment in silence.

Then Sam yelled, "Wow! Did you see that?"

"Holy shit. They're out there." Jeff added with a big grin.

Charged with the thrill of the hunt, we reassembled the rigging and started trolling again.

Our lucky streak continued with two similar displays in the afternoon. One blue tail-walker looked about eight feet long. The other was smaller. Both had tossed our hooks. The novelty of watching big fish thrash around had worn off. It was time to keep one.

After lunch we spotted Minke whales in the distance. As their spouts and bounding fins approached, we realized they were after our bait. The thought of being hauled around by a frantic whale jolted us into action once again. There wasn't time to get the lines in, so Sam jammed the throttles down to escape. When the boat went up onto a plane, so did the live mackerel on our hooks. As if they weren't having a hard enough day, the poor little guys had to water ski until the cetaceans were at a safe distance.

196

At four o'clock, we turned for home, disappointed, but kept the lines out, just in case. At 4:25, the port outrigger snapped free. The reel screeched as the whizzing line spun out at twice its previous speed. Jeff grabbed the rod, yelling, "We've got a big one!"

Dorji and I broke down the outriggers and quickly wound in the empty lines. As the fish raced around, Jeff shouted commands to Sam, "Forward slow . . . forward fast . . . neutral . . . back! back! back! Forward fast . . . steer to port . . . neutral . . . " as he alternately wound and let spin. It was a hell of a fight for twenty minutes, and when it tail-walked, it looked over ten feet long.

The wild maneuvering ended abruptly when the giant fish dove. The angle on the outgoing line dropped gradually until it pointed straight down. The high speed express was on its way, but where would it stop? We were over the Palau Trench. There was no bottom for 20,000 feet. Fearing the light sixty-pound-test monofilament would break, Jeff eased the drag off slightly. Even then, the reel was heating up fast, forcing us to douse it with water. There was no point in running the engines, so the boat was adrift, rising and falling slowly on the gentle swells.

As the reels diminished in size, Jeff asked, "Are we gonna keep it?"

"Hell, yes!"

"Get the leaders from two of those rods attached to this reel. Clip the leaders in right here on either side."

Quickly, we readied the new rods for the load. When there was a few hundred yards of line left, Jeff slipped the rod butt out of the chest harness.

"When I say three, go."

He counted, "One, two, three," cranked the drag to full, and watched seven-hundred dollars of his fishing gear plunge overboard. Now two reels were spinning, and there was still no sign of stopping the beast.

Jeff noted that there was over a half mile of line out. "We're gonna be here for awhile."

Ten minutes later, the fish started slowing down. It was a seven-hundred-dollar bet. Should we crank the drag up and save Jeff's gear by snapping the lower line, or run it out to the bitter end? The owner said go for it. The reels were each a few yards short of empty when the behemoth finally stopped. Jeff estimated 3,500 feet of line out below us. It was five-thirty.

Sam was supposed to pick up his wife at the airport at seven o'clock. Oh, well. We had priorities.

With one rod on each side of the boat, the colossal tension bent the tips into the water. Even with full drag, we had to keep our thumbs mashed onto the reels to hold them. We'd crank in a foot, then the reels would slip, letting a few inches back out.

An hour later, we saw Sam's wife's plane, silhouetted against the sunset as it approached the runway. The lights of Koror appeared on the horizon. I took a compass heading on them and got ready for a long night. Fortunately it was calm. Any wind chop could have bounced the boat enough to break the thin line. We wound, chatted, and drank beer under the stars. At ten-thirty, whales passed close enough to spray us with their spouts. Whales have very bad breath.

At midnight, there was a major crisis: no more beer.

At one a.m., it started to rain hard, which wasn't at all fun in the open boat. I borrowed a windbreaker, huddled in the driest wet spot under the captain's chair, and managed to get a little sleep as the rain danced off my back. When Jeff's rod came aboard at two a.m., they cheered. I woke up and joined them. The rain had stopped, and we could see boat lights in the distance. Someone shot a flare. They were searching for us. Unfortunately, we hadn't thought to bring a flashlight. We didn't have running lights or a radio, either. After a couple of hours, our friends gave up and went home. I went back to sleep.

At three-thirty, the guys rousted me so they could sleep. I sat down on the rod handle and cranked steadily by myself. The next three hours passed quickly as I became entranced in routine. There were no other sounds except the clicking of the reel and the occasional whir of line slipping back out under tension. As the reel filled, I knew I was getting close. Soon after the pre-dawn light began to define shapes in the boat, the steel leader came up. I looked down and saw a huge dark spot in the crystal clear water. The fish hung lifeless, tail-wrapped three times on the thin cable leader.

My yell jolted the guys awake. Four of us had no trouble hauling it aboard by its bill. As soon as it was in the boat, we all fell back and looked at the monster. We were hungry, tired, and emotionally spent. Even with gloves on, the powerful cranking had ground the skin out of the palms of our hands.

Our biggest concern was to get back and let everyone know we were all right. Back at the dock, a dozen friends were loading boats and organizing plans to hunt the open ocean for us. Apparently, the search efforts were about to explode to enormous proportions, involving aircraft and a flotilla of volunteers. As we approached, the sight of a huge bill and tail hanging over the sides of our boat explained all. Sam was forgiven when his wife ran down the gangplank and leaped into his arms. Cameras appeared. Breakfast and coffee materialized for us. We told the story through mouthfuls of much needed nutrition before taking our trophy over to fisheries for a weigh in. It tipped the scales at 317 pounds and measured 11.5 feet stem to stern.

We made the front page of the local paper, and days later, people I didn't even know were stopping me on the street to hear the story. The best part, however, was the steaks. The marlin had four columns of muscle that ran the length of its body in their respective quadrants. Each was over a foot in diameter at its fattest point. As each column was sectioned, inch thick slabs rolled away from the knife like warm butter. We barbecued and feasted on the best fish I've ever laid taste buds on. We gave everyone enough to last for days and sold the rest to local restaurants.

That's my one and only "fish story."

ENZO
Palau

"You know it's been a good vacation when it takes all of your willpower to leave." Max

Two Germans chartered McCready's sailboat and hired me as their private guide. I called one of them Enzo because of his jovial barrel-chested resemblance to Jean Reno's character in "The Big Blue." He had a five-day growth on his face, and the crewcut on his balding head wasn't much longer. Max, his sidekick and understudy, was frail in comparison. Enzo had five-hundred very deep dives logged. Max had a hundred.

When we met, they said, "We want to dive deep."

"No problem."

I always liked working with McCready. His spacious forty-eight footer had a compressor, a barbecue for fresh fish, and two coolers stuffed with beer. Instead of returning to town every night, we stayed out in the rock islands for days. With the Germans, we were four. We offered them unlimited diving: "Just say when and where."

"When" turned out to be five times a day including a night dive.

"Where" was far below the normal dive sites.

I liked these guys. They didn't mess around.

Few had seen the sections of reef we explored, way down deep. Twenty-foot strands of resilient wire coral stuck straight out from the wall every few feet. Virtual thickets of see-through fans, some over ten-feet across, were aligned perpendicular to the current, and there were dozens of new nooks and caves. The visibility stayed around 200 feet that week, allowing us to look up and still be able to see the reef towering above.

Big Dropoff was our deepest sojourn to the nether region. I called that dive the Chuck Yeager dive, because at 207 feet, the water below us was as black as the outer space that Yeager had for sky when he flew to the top of the atmosphere. The black below faded gradually upwards to indigo, navy, and finally the light blues of the water above. As far as we could see to either side, the wall was dead vertical and completely flat, which gave us the flipped-sideways illusion of it being the bottom. While stoned to the gills on narcosis, I remember my air tasting cool and pleasantly sweet.

I thought the boys might like a different type of deep adventure, so I took them to the cave behind the Blue Holes. The site gets its name from four round openings in the reef above a huge chasm. This grotto, when lit by shafts of sunlight from the holes, is one of the world's best dives – especially when the water clarity is superb. At eighty feet, there is a small cave entrance. I had once squeezed through it and found a string from the original exploration leading back into the darkness. I moved along it until I could barely see the blue light from the entrance, then stopped, afraid of getting lost. I couldn't see a thing around me with my small dive light because the cave was huge. Only the white string was visible as it disappeared into unknown depths. I knew that I had to come back and find out where it went. With Enzo and Max, I had the perfect opportunity.

The two of them were equipped with high-tech underwater lights, each brighter than an automobile headlight. To match them, I loaded up with as many D-cell lamps as I could find, intending to light the cave up like daytime. It worked. The tunnel had an arched ceiling and a 120-foot deep sandy bottom throughout. It was sixty feet high on the average and almost as wide. We measured our course with compasses and were surprised to find that the cave went along the reef, rather than back into it. At an average depth of 100 feet, the string ran over 200 yards to a dead end. The tunnel was not a normal limestone cave. Instead, it appeared to be a fluke in the coral. Perhaps it had been an underwater gully, over which coral had grown to form a roof.

After a five minute swim in, and another five minutes out, we were greeted back into the world of light by the fantastic scenery under the blue holes. We swam through the lower exit to the outside of the reef and let the current shoot us down to Blue Corner where we were soon surrounded by dozens of sharks. When we worked up the reef for a long safety stop in twenty feet of water, we surprised a leopard shark lying in a sand hole. Its angular spotted torso gracefully swung back and forth as it swam away. Max tapped me on the shoulder and pointed. We had also barged in on a mating pair of turtles. A smaller turtle was lying on the back of a larger one, giving us a "can you please go away" look. Why? His extended tail was rammed into the backside of the female — and what a tail it was! The part I saw was thicker than a papaya. I was envious.

On surfacing, Max yelled, "Affengeil!"

Enzo yelled, "Spitze! Das war wunderschön! Out of five hundred dives, that was the best!"

The boys were happy, and that's what we like. Satisfied customers and great dives.

ﻼ ﻼ ﻼ

Back on the boat, we noticed whale spouts a few miles out to sea and motored out to them. The spouts were shooting forward at forty-five degree angles. They were sperm whales! We got right in among them and counted five. The closest one, longer than our forty-eight foot boat, floated calmly, ignoring us. We jumped in with masks and saw why. The leviathan was chewing on giant squid. As we approached, it swam lazily down and away at an angle, leaving partially masticated tentacles with handball-sized suckers spinning in its wake. (Sperm whales hunt giant squid to the depth of one mile, using sonar to probe the darkness. They can stay under water for up to ninety minutes on one dive.)

We climbed back aboard, and McCready headed for the next whale. As we pulled alongside, it lifted its head out of the water to see what we looked like above the surface. We were eye-to-eye, separated by twenty feet. It gave us the once over, then raised its massive flukes ten feet out of the water as it sounded.

ಶಿ ಶಿ ಶಿ

Enzo was quite a character. During one decompression stop, he gave me a series of hand signals that meant "my computer says it's time to go up and drink beer." Later, on the boat, actually drinking a beer, he expounded on the subject. "You know when the computer says three minute stop at ten feet? It means the computer has to stay down, not you. You can come up and drink beer."

Max nodded in agreement. I laughed. They didn't. Now, I'm not sure if they were joking or not.

After our last dive, Max asked if I had noticed the magnet in his luggage. I hadn't, and apparently, I wasn't supposed to. His computer wasn't designed to go deeper than 160 feet, so after every deeper dive, it would go into twenty-four hour lockout, becoming useless. This safety feature was installed to keep the diver out of the water for a day. Max's solution? Put it next to a strong magnet to erase the memory and restart it before the next dive. The drawback was that any record of body nitrogen from previous dives was lost. In effect, he had reduced his high-tech instrument to a digital timer and depth gauge. I suddenly realized why he always stayed so close to Enzo. He was relying on the other computer to keep from getting bent.

Das ist wahnsinn, Max. You nut.

SOUTHEAST ASIA

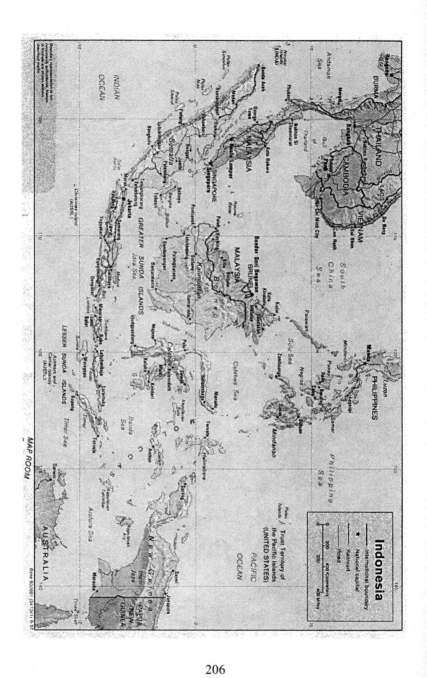

206

GREEN FOREST, GREEN FLASH
Koh Pha Ngan, Thailand

"Where there's life, there's hope." Barton

"'Have a drink,' said Harry looking out across the gray swell of the gulf stream where the round red sun was just touching the water. 'Watch that. When she goes all the way under it'll turn bright green.'" Papa

February 2, 1996

Jungle. The word conjures up images of strange and deadly animals, odd noises, voracious mosquitoes, thickets of undergrowth, pith helmets, and machetes. In reality, large animals and impassable masses of vegetation aren't encountered any more than in American forests. There are fewer pesky insects than expected. (Summertime in Florida is far worse.) One thing holds true, however. If it's not windy, the jungle is damn hot.

It's called a rain forest for a reason. Low-pressure monsoon conditions give the landscape the ultimate soak. These depressing wet and windy periods are the only time the tropics feel cold. More commonly, rain comes from brief localized thunderstorms that interrupt the heat and boosts the spirits with a refreshing half-hour shower. Unfortunately, humidity soars when the sunlight returns — a good time to be under water.

Tropical forests display a variety of personalities. Some thrive year round in relentless humidity. With no winter, the interminable theme is GROW. Whatever can take root, will. The variety of leaf shapes says it all: spiked, rounded, jagged, smooth, rubbery, delicate, crenate.

At the edges of the equatorial belt, there is a winter dry season. During this drought, the lower islands of Indonesia turn dusty, the hills of Saint Lucia turn a tawny hue, and cactuses in the Virgin Islands find their niche on sunny south-facing slopes. I enjoy them all, but my favorite is the jungle of Palau because it has a feature that I haven't seen anywhere else — it glows in the dark.

At night, on the pitch-dark floor of the Palauan rain forest, dim green patches of bioluminescent fungus show up on branches, logs, and tree trunks, creating a crisscrossing three-dimensional pattern of barely visible light. An occasional firefly adds motion to the scene. When the moon comes up, the shadows are still inky black, but white speckles appear where thin beams infiltrate the matted canopy of leaves above.

On all tropical islands, shorelines are the domain of the coconut palm, a tree with the ability to lean out over the water for unobstructed sunlight and drop coconuts that can float away and reproduce on distant shores.

Young green coconuts full of sweet effervescent milk are the tropical refreshment of choice. The meat is thin, creamy, and easily scooped out with a "spoon" hacked from the husk with a machete.

Climbing the slippery vertical trunks of coconut palms demands concentration. The most common technique is to grab the tree, lean back, and shuffle feet up the stalk. Others vary by region: Saint Lucians prefer to climb in thick-soled boots. Samoans tie their T-shirts in a loop across their bare feet, creating a friction strap that allows them to stand on the bark. Micronesians cheat by cutting steps. Thai people don't bother with ascents. They have a small army of trained monkeys that twist the nuts off while their trainers wait on the ground, yelling commands and keeping a grip on their very long leash.

I also love the sounds of a jungle, particularly the ones around my bungalow here on Pha Ngan Island. Some birds twitter while others chortle in falling tones. A little brown bird sounds like it is speaking Thai when it warbles, "Der diao diao" (wait, wait). Yellow-billed mockingbirds imitate those not in attendance.

Cicadas cluster together in large trees at dusk to form an orchestra pit in the amphitheater of branches. When the players are in position, the conductor raises his baton and cues the musicians into action with a rising Braaap. The percussion section sounds like a bunch of old crackers playing combs on the front porch of an Appalachian cabin. The string section sounds like a cluster of cars with drained batteries trying to start. The horn section sets up an unfaltering blare. After a few minutes of loudly showing off, there is a decrescendo as some of the players sit back, rest, and allow the occupants of the first chairs do their solos. After several more minutes, they join in for a finale. With a final wave of the baton, the tree goes silent.

After the cicadas' performance, other creatures show off their vocal talents. One unidentifiable insect lets go with a steady siren-like ring for minutes on end. Tree frogs cluck in tweets. Small geckos chirp, but the larger tokays announce themselves with a loud "ho-kay, ho-kay, ho-kay," hence their name. With a little imagination, an F and U can be heard in each retort, making it sound like the critter is dishing out the ultimate insult. Suddenly, with a rev, the conductor strikes up the cicada band into an encore performance of "Dueling Helicopters." Their rendition brings a tear to my eye.

&ep; &ep; &ep;

The sunset right now is developing nicely. Below the porch of my bungalow, the wanna-be waves of the lagoon are lapping intermittently against the sandy shore. The shallow water leading out to the reef is powder blue over the white sand bottom. Farther out, a spilled candle wax pattern of chestnut coral blends into the broad band of brown over the reef. At the far edge of the coral, real waves break in ranks. Beyond, the deep blue of the open sea is split by a brilliant golden path of twinkling, mesmerizing flickers that leads to the sinking fireball in the west. Distant cumulus clouds are radiating pastel pinks, lavenders, and yellows. One dark thunderhead is making the water below it glow green. Forked lightning flashes down from it, stinging the horizon every minute or so.

Looking down the beach, I notice that nobody else shares my interest. They are occupied with books, conversations, or naps. Don't they know that the end of every day holds the potential for a magical event, the "green flash?" The name is inaccurate; it is not a flash — only the color change that the sun occasionally goes through during the final instant of the day. As the last bit of the solar orb disappears over the horizon, the orange transforms for a full second into a brilliant spot of emerald green as it refracts through the atmosphere. (In Palau, we often saw this effect in sapphire blue.) It is best seen over water when there are no clouds in the distance.

Well, it's time. The sun has hit the horizon, but I'm not looking at it yet. If I do, I'll get spots in my eyes and won't be able to tell if there is a flash or not. Using my peripheral vision, I wait until there are only a few seconds left. I look and . . . there it is — a fleeting speck of green. . . . To think it's wintertime at home right now.

THE COMMISSIONER OF OATS
Gili Air, Indonesia (Thailand, Malaysia)

"Indonesians are very caring and try to be helpful to tourists. They just can't figure out how to do it right." Lynne

September 4, 1996

Greetings from non-sequitur hell. Saying "no" in Southeast Asia is the ultimate social sin – it is considered rude to be so blunt. Instead, when the locals can't answer a question, they end up generating confusion. I'm convinced that they are intentionally collaborating to drive me and every other visitor crazy by any means necessary.

The Indonesian waiters at the restaurant next to the dive shop are part of this conspiracy, but I have been around long enough to catch on to their three favorite tricks: the yes answer, the nonsense answer, and answering a question with a nonsense question.

An example of the yes answer is this:

"Which way is it to the harbor?"

"Yes"

"The harbor. Where the boats are. Do you know what I mean?"

"Yes."

"I mean, is it (pointing) this way, or this way?"

"Yes."

"Where do <u>you</u> get on the boat when you leave?"

"Yes."

An example of the nonsense answer is this:

"One spaghetti marinara, please."

"We don't have any papayas yet."

"What do papayas have to do with anything?"

"We only serve fresh fruit."

And last, the nonsense question:

"One iced tea and one club sandwich, please."

"Tea or coffee?"

"Iced tea, with lemon."

"Rice?"

"Ice, and one club sandwich" (sitting alone).

"One or two?"

"One. Do you have french fries today?"

"Are you diving later?"

Since I'm a regular, they have to come up with new diversions on a daily basis. Yesterday, as I was eating lunch, I ordered something else to drink. "One Coke, please."

Five minutes later, the manager came up and asked, "You want to use the kitchen?"

"What?"

"You want to make something for yourself?"

"Uh . . . no."

"The waiter said you want to cook."

"I don't want to <u>cook</u>. I want a <u>Coke</u>."

Most service-oriented workers in Indonesia try hard to deliver — sometimes too hard. For example, waiters won't say, "I am sorry, we are out of banana shakes, would you like a papaya shake instead?" They take the order and let the customer sit for an hour while kids are sent on a search mission for ripe bananas. No matter how many times I beg them to just say no, they never do.

Before, if I waited more than twenty minutes to be served, I would ask waiters to check my order. The standard answer was always "coming, coming." It didn't take long to figure out that "coming, coming" meant the order might arrive on the table sometime before the next lunar eclipse. Now, I check the pantry for ingredients before I ask for anything.

If I didn't have a sense of humor, they would have won long ago. I was last put to the test on Komodo Island (home of the dragons). I had seated myself in the only restaurant just before noon.

The waitress strolled up with a happy smile. "May I help you?"

"Yes, I'll have a fried rice, please."

"We don't have fried rice now."

"Okay. How about fried noodles?"

"We're not serving fried noodles either."

"What do you have?"

"We're not serving anything."

"Why not?"

"The cook doesn't work when he's eating lunch."

"Right. Then I'll just have a beer and wait for the cook to finish."

"The cook has the key to the refrigerator."

"Oh. What are you doing, then?"

"I'm working."

"But the restaurant isn't open."

"Yes it is. Can you come back in twenty minutes?"

Never forget. Those who prepare your food always have the upper hand.

&❦ &❦ &❦

The citizens of Georgetown (Penang), Malaysia were merciless one morning as I wandered the town with a legal document that needed to be notarized. I set out with a helpful man's pencil mark on my map but couldn't find anything resembling a notary. I tried the tourist information bureau where I found a man who spoke English.

"Can you please help me? I'm looking for a notary public."

"See the immigration building across the street? Go around the corner and through the first door on the right."

"Thank you very much."

That was easy. I happily went through the first door on the right and found myself standing in a public toilet. I couldn't help but laugh out loud. Guys! A notary public is not a place to piss.

Back on the street, I asked an intelligent-looking gentleman, "Excuse me, I'm looking for a notary public."

"There's one next to the bank over there."

"Thanks."

I scoured all of the adjacent buildings, but didn't find anything.

I asked inside the bank. "I understand that there's a notary public nearby. Can you tell me where?"

"We don't have a notary here. This is a bank."

"Yes I know, but is there one next door maybe?"

"Do you know the address?"

"No"

"May I see your passport?"

What did my passport have to do with anything? I was obviously dealing with professionals, so I said, "Never mind," and beat a retreat.

Near the post office, an Indian man with a heavy accent explained that notary publics were commonly called "Commissioners of Oats," but didn't know where one was. I set off again looking for a Commissioner of Oats, wondering where the term came from. Since Malaysia was once a British colony, I figured it went back to the middle ages in England where a guy with a ledger sat around watching carts full of grain go by.

After forty-five minutes of weary plodding in the heat, I was finally directed to a Commissioner of Oats. As I sat at his desk, I had to laugh again. There was a framed document on the wall certifying him as a "Commissioner of Oaths."

WELCOME TO THE THIRD WORLD
Gili Air, Indonesia

"Watch their eyes." Bill, preparing me for Indonesia

August 30, 1996

Indonesian National Airlines Flight 7 approaches the runway. Instead of a smooth landing, the plane hits with a jolt that knocks a few oxygen masks out of the overhead compartments. The pilot hits the throttle during the bounce and takes off again. After a lazy circle, the plane comes banging down again, almost hard enough to knock out dental fillings. The plane goes around again. After the third approach, the pilot shoots a normal landing and taxis to the terminal.

"What was that all about?"

"The nose gear gets stuck sometimes, so we have to knock it down before we can land."

Bali! I've finally made it — an island of towering volcanoes, rice-terraced hills, architectural fantasy, and beautiful women — a bastion of Hinduism amidst a nation of Muslims. I admire this verdant paradise briefly through an arrival hall window before noticing that my entire flight has gotten in line ahead of me. I have to wait thirty minutes for everyone else to disappear through the doors to customs before I can get my passport stamped.

After I hand it over to a young mustached officer, he asks, "Where is your return plane ticket?"

"I don't have one. The embassy in Singapore told me it was no longer necessary."

He eyes me coldly and drops my passport into his shirt pocket. I suddenly feel very alone in the stone foyer.

"Come with me," he says as he steps out from his cubicle.

"Is there a problem?"

He ignores me and heads for an officious looking side door. He holds it open as I follow him into a small room with bad lighting. Behind the only desk is an older officer smoking a cigarette while doing his best Pancho Villa.

He waves at an empty chair. "Have a seat, please."

The young guy shuts the door behind us and says a few words to the plump desk jockey in Behasa Malay.

El capitan holds his gaze on me as he rocks back in his chair.

His hands come together over the papers on the desktop, touching only at the finger tips. "We're deporting you."

I remember my friend's advice and look at their eyes. They look back at me like a couple of playground bullies after my lunch money. I know they're up to something.

"Is there any way I can avoid being deported?"

"How much money do you have?"

"About 700 dollars."

"How do you expect to survive in Bali on 700 dollars? You want a sixty-day visa?"

"Friends of mine told me that they got by for less than ten dollars a day here."

"Ten dollars? Impossible. Let us see your money."

Thinking they're going to count it, I dig it out of my money belt and hold it up like a poker hand.

The young one snatches out a crisp twenty and says, "Welcome to our country."

That was three months ago. Now I'm working full time on Gili Air, the smallest of the Gili Islands, and have learned a hell of a lot more about this crazy land. There is a point where bribery becomes extortion. Instead of submitting an offering to speed things up a bit, people suddenly find themselves paying to get out of a jam that officials have forced them into. This is what lubricates the gears of the Indonesian government.

The government builds roads, schools, and hospitals, and that's about it. The older and usually richer men control the local politics of the villages — a regional "Mafia" for every hundred square miles. What the government deems lawful or not in court is irrelevant. The "Mafia" also takes the punishment of local small-time criminals into their own hands, and they don't mess around either. Here is an example: three thieves from Lombok were caught stealing Walkmans and cameras from tourist bungalows on the Gili Islands. The people on Lombok are Sasak and speak Sasak. The Gili Islanders are descendants of Sulawesi pirates and speak a completely different dialect. A message had to be sent to anybody else contemplating a burglary. "Don't mess around with our bread and butter." Instead of involving the police, the islanders beat the thieves badly. One died. The other two were hospitalized.

The regular police are generally incapable stooges, so if justice needs to be carried out, the military police are called in. They show up in plain clothes, survey the situation, pass judgment, and carry out a sentence. The commonest solution is to cart the offenders out into the jungle and pop bullets through their heads. When they are finished, the original victim's family pays them off with a generous gratuity. I suspect that the military police had something to do with the five dissidents found dead in a river during the recent Jakarta riots. The government claimed they drowned. I don't think any Indonesians would argue if they were told that the rioters were shot before they went swimming.

The smartest guy around was the restaurant manager, Adi, so I asked him what he thought of the riots. He said not to worry because the army was strong enough to put down any revolt. That wasn't exactly the answer I wanted. I was after a political discussion, but found out that his was a typical local attitude towards politics. I see the advantage now of staying on this island in my hammock, listening to the birds and sound of the waves, and ignoring everything else.

Backwoods illegal activity is permitted as long as it doesn't upset the local leadership. For example, dynamiting fishing is outlawed, but common in these islands. On most dives, I have to lead divers across a lunar landscape patches of algae-covered rubble that was once a flourishing reef. Occasionally, we'll be jolted by sharp concussions under water from the blasts, and I'll need to explain to my new students what is going on. It doesn't take an economist to figure out that these islands will thrive on dive tourism instead of rubbery fish exports. I know I'm only a guest in their country, but I did try to get a word in with the villains when I met them briefly.

I made it a point to ask, "Do you cut down trees to get coconuts? Do you eat a chicken that lays eggs? Why are you demolishing the reef? Leave something for your children."

They smiled and said, "Yes," giving me the brush-off.

Those were hard topics to talk about with the locals. I had better conversations discussing the "wonders" of western civilization. I explained microwave ovens and microwave popcorn to Adi and the restaurant staff for fifteen minutes one evening. I also managed to convince them that people in America went to supermarkets to buy dog food and cat food in cans. Though they seemed to believe that, they were dubious when I said that animals were kept inside the house sometimes. I didn't bother trying to tell them about pet psychiatrists and doggie day care. They would have written me off as a nut case.

My biggest challenge has been adapting to the strange ways of this little island, a problem worsened by the influence of my Swiss heritage. Swiss people make precision timepieces. The guys here go until something breaks or crashes. "What" and "if" do not occur naturally together in any question. Carefree transforms into careless as soon as the morning whistle blows. This is a place where things don't go right . . . or wrong. They just happen. Whether the results work or not, I have to admire the ways in which they are attempted. Whether it's auto mechanics using a stick from the side of the road, or a brainless attempt to fill a coke bottle from a bucket without a funnel, I get a laugh out of the situation . . . eventually.

Let's take for example, the topic of the Indonesian national tool — the hammer. Hammers are useful for driving screws, digging, breaking wires, punching holes, or trying to get the valves off scuba tanks. When a hammer isn't available, anything that can be used for pounding such as a rock, bottle, or wrench, can substitute. Part of the problem is that no one has ever taught these guys how to do things right. They grew up watching their parents acting like the Keystone Kops around western technology, so it doesn't bother them to pound on bent nails until they barely hold and then walk away. I asked a guy in Bali for a screw once, and he went over and backed one out of the floorboard of a car. I asked if he needed it, and he said no, there were still three screws holding the floor plate.

One afternoon, I watched the construction of a small house near the dive shop. The workers furiously hammered together a wooden framework, stood it on short posts, then haphazardly nailed thatched siding and grass roofing onto it. When it was finished, they put a foundation in by ramming red bricks, cinder blocks, and stones under the lowest beams. I didn't want to point out that the rest of the world builds foundations first, then houses.

I think I've figured out why they do this. 120 calories per hour are required for a human brain to actively operate. This can add up to a reasonable portion of the body's total energy output in this lackadaisical environment, so they respond by going into mental hibernation. I've watched the dive shop staff sweep dirt onto customers' feet, run boats aground in calm conditions, and hook up scuba gear backwards after years of practice. I have also worked out the signs for coasting in neutral. If they're smiling, look out! There's nothing like a big reassuring grin to give away the fact that they're not on the ball.

The Sasaks I work with (The Gili Islanders don't work in the dive business) are friendly, ultra-laid-back, and fun to joke around with. For me, it is high school revisited.

Here is the cast:

-Adi is the manager of the restaurant next to the dive shop, as well as the island's most vicious chess player.
-Rudy is the beach-party guitarist and the only waiter who has a semblance of a brain in the restaurant other than Adi.

-Max is a boat boy and is not really named Max, but I call him Max because he calls me Max because he thinks that's my name.

-Rose is the nubile cutie working as a waitress in another restaurant across the field. The village headman is trying to add her as his sixth wife, but she has a crush on me. Every time she smiles, blushes, and waves at me from the restaurant, I fear that the headman is going to kick me off the island, or worse.

-Suno works and lives in the dive shop. He is also a kindhearted mystic, easily upset by evil doings, and able to soothe painful injuries with a simple touch.

When I first arrived, I tried to work with the staff as fellow employees. This soon turned into a major source of entertainment called "stand around and watch Mike work." It didn't take long to figure out that the only possible role for me in the dive shop was lord, master, and overall son-of-a-bitch. I banned littering on the floor, sleeping on the couches while customers were in the shop, and had the neighborhood kids thrown out (Damn it, Jim. This is a dive business, not an orphanage).

One of my first obstacles was communication. Every morning, the employees would barrage me with non-sequiturs, incorrectly repeat what I'd say, and answer questions with questions until I wanted to kill. The solution was to delegate authority so I promoted Suno to lieutenant. My junior officer seized the reins of his command with a fervor, barking orders like the Sasak version of Patton. Supreme Headquarters Allied Powers Gili Air became my hammock in the corner of the shop. From there, I directed operations with the wave of a finger.

Early one morning, I went into work and was surprised by a man doing something in the gear-rinse water basin. I walked over to find him washing a wooden chicken cage with a chicken inside.

"Chicken take bath!" He smiled proudly.

The once fresh water was clouded with dirt, chicken crap, and feathers. I didn't say anything to the man, but I did let out a yell for Suno. When he showed up, I passed the "no chicken washing in the dive shop" rule.

I'm on a small flat island covered in trees, surrounded by reefs, ringed with beaches, and built up for backpacking tourists. Walking the perimeter takes an hour if I don't stop to chat. A village with 200 inhabitants is in the middle and tourist bungalows line the beaches. There are a dozen bad restaurants and two or three good ones. Pine, palm, and papaya trees sway lazily in the sun, and that's all the island has to offer. I'm here to sell the tourists dive courses.

Other than the occasional alpenglow sunset on Rinjani volcano in the distance, people offer the only change in scenery. Women walk past balancing pots or baskets on their heads; their saronged hips sway as their bare feet pat through the dirt. There is often a clue as to what they are transporting, like a mahi-mahi fish tail sticking out from under a lid. Men shuttle bricks or cement up from the beach on balanced shoulder sticks. (Wheelbarrow? . . . Anyone? . . . Anyone?) Barefoot and bare chested, they wear *only* a sarong. Children wander freely, often wearing nothing. Horse carts, the only vehicles, knock up clouds of dust as they rattle around the "superhighway" that rings the island.

The women are somewhat shy and completely unavailable. Because of the Islamic religion, sex before marriage is strictly taboo. Arranged marriages are common, so free courtship rarely exists. Local men and women never touch or kiss in public. For a woman to sit in my hammock with me would be far too risqué. Even if I bring a woman from Bali or Lombok over, I'd still get kicked off the island.

Since my arrival three months ago, I have become more and more lackadaisical. The ability to use words longer than two syllables in a sentence has disappeared. The Australians know all about this condition. It is called, "Going Troppo." If someone has gone Troppo, it means they have been in the heat too long and can no longer be trusted to handle sharp objects, heavy machinery, or caustic substances. To avoid this problem with their nation's leaders, the Aussies established their first capital in a cool climate (Melbourne). Unfortunately, the only cool climates in Indonesia are on top of the volcanoes. I'm trying to combat the onslaught of this condition by keeping my mind active with crosswords, chess, and conversations with educated tourists. Unfortunately, I'm fighting a losing battle.

I'm reaching the end of another vicious evening cycle of drink-the-beer-before-it-gets-warm. I don't usually drink so much, but it's so goddamned dull here at night that I run out of things to keep me active. The major excitement at the moment is waiting to see if the big gecko on the wall is going to eat the moth that is crawling around near it.

Adi's restaurant is playing Rod Stewart's Greatest Hits for the fifth time today. Pretty soon, they'll put on their other tape, The Best of Bryan Adams. The electrical generator next door is not quite loud enough to drown out the Do Ya Think I'm Sexy song. I think I'll sneak out tonight and steal the muffler.

I didn't have any divers today, but the day wasn't a total loss. My big accomplishment was teaching tricks to the flies that were stuck in the flypaper. I amused myself for almost a minute with this dialogue: "Oh, hello. Welcome to the party. Stick around for awhile. Hah! Sit. Good boy. Now, shake hands. Oh, you can't. Your little leg is stuck. Okay, now lie down. Roll over. Good boy, now play dead."

Day-to-day life is unpredictable here. It's like the wild west, except that it won't be tamed anytime soon. Every now and then I'll see something that just doesn't register. For example, I saw a woman picking through her baby's hair for lice when I first arrived (a common sight here), but didn't think anything of it until I saw her find one, toss it between her teeth, chomp it, and eat it. My brain seized-up in a loop for a few minutes, trying to match the data input with a Jane Goodall documentary, but was unable to find an appropriate slot.

A similar experience happened last week at a store near the dive shop. As I was walking to dinner, I glanced over to my right and saw a monkey screwing a cat. My brain didn't register that either, so I walked several steps before looking back in awe. Sure enough, my eyes were not faulty. A male monkey was mounted up, straddling a cat from behind that was twice his size. The feline was lying prone and looking indifferent. The monkey bared his teeth at me, so I guessed he wanted privacy and kept walking. (He must have been desperate for some pussy.)

I promised my friends I'd leave before they had to come get me. It may be too late. I know it has been too long because:

- I stopped noticing women carrying everything around on their heads;
- I started wearing a sarong around in public like everyone else instead of shorts;
- it seems normal that the only form of transportation is a horse cart;
- I've gotten used to the heat rash in my armpits;
- the bathing routine is hand-drawing water from the well to dump over myself;
- when I have guests, I serve meals on newspapers spread on the floor;
- sitting on my haunches has become easy;
- it is standard to use soap and water instead of toilet paper, and;
- I use the local technique of eating rice with my hands.

Another giveaway is I spend more time in my hammock than diving, and my coworkers don't drive me nuts anymore when they bang the outboard propeller along the reef to get six feet closer to the beach before raising the engine.

There are a few cultural obstacles that I can't surmount. The most aggravating is that everyone chews with open mouths, forcing me to pick up my plate at mealtimes and flee. Another is that the men often hold hands or put their arms around each other. That's fine until they try to get me involved. I can handle an arm on my shoulder, but I draw the line at hand holding. There's also a lack of respect for personal space. I'm particularly miffed about this at the moment because there is a man staring transfixed at his own reflection in my sunglasses. It wouldn't be such a bad thing except that I happen to be wearing them, and he's literally in my face. I've ignored him long enough. He's still here. I gotta go.

223

NATURE'S CALL
Gili Air, Indonesia

"Mongo only pawn . . . in game of life." Mongo

The Asian style toilet is a challenge foreign visitors. The top of the oval porcelain basin is flush with a concrete step that elevates it four inches above the floor. A water filled drain is in the rear of the target area. Grip marks for the feet are embossed in the ceramic on either side. Careful balance is needed while squatting over the narrow receptacle. Nearby is a tub full of water with a plastic scoop bowl floating inside. This utilitarian pseudo-bucket is primarily used to hand flush the commode and wash backsides, but is also used to take "showers" with.

Welcome to the third world. Unhygienic restaurant kitchens abound. Consequently, I've got the Hershey squirts so bad, there's no time to argue. Wake up, go straight outside, and leave a little present on the path. The local outhouse is too far away from my grass hut.

It's pitch black because there's no moon, and all the generators have been shut off for the night. After decorating the dirt trail, I'm in dire need to clean up. Back in the bungalow, I fumble blindly until I find a flashlight. I flick the switch and nothing happens. Damn it. Why can't they make durable batteries in this country?

I bump into my watch and use its tiny blue light to locate a lighter. Ahh, light! − well until it starts to burn my thumb anyway. Toilet paper? Just ran out. Soap? The rats have dragged it away again.

Shampoo is the logical solution, and I snatch the bottle up before tearing out the door for the latrine because nature is calling again. There's no time to search for a sarong, so I run buck naked through the sleeping village. I burst through the door, and somehow manage to drop the lighter into the water basin. I have to squat and aim for the commode in absolute darkness. I manage successfully and then grope around for the hand bucket, fill it, and pour water into the toilet to flush it. As a perfect conclusion, I feel liquid from the clogged drain overflowing on to my bare feet.

"Shit."

❧ ❧ ❧

Underwater emergencies are handled easily unless you are leading a group of divers. The "wait here" hand signal is an important part of any third world dive briefing. Amazingly, my divers have never figured out why I've left them alone for a couple minutes. Either that, or they've been too polite to mention it.

I found myself in dire straits once because I was wearing a wetsuit. As the last diver boarded the boat, I descended twenty-five feet to the bottom, took off my BC, draped my weights over my shoulder, unzipped my suit and pulled it down around my knees. Relief!

Unfortunately, my power inflator stuck open after being bumped. As my BC filled with air and floated, my regulator dragged me to the surface by my teeth. Nobody mentioned that, either.

I always say that you can do anything under water. If you haven't tried this yet, don't be bashful. The fish will love you for it.

THE BENDS
Gili Air, Indonesia

"The first symptom is denial." Dan, a Diver's Alert Network physician

September 5th

I'm lying here immobile because of severe stabbing pain in my right ankle. Two hours after yesterday's last dive, a hint of discomfort appeared. I didn't think anything of it until it intensified enough to make me limp home from dinner. At 4 a.m. this morning, the pain woke me up. I was pinned to my bed in agony, unable to walk. After sunrise, I made it twenty feet over to the hammock with an oar for a crutch and a handful of painkillers. I haven't moved since. Some purple discoloration has appeared around the ball of the joint, but strangely, there is no swelling. Are air bubbles rupturing blood vessels in my ankle?

The last dive was an unavoidable reverse profile and included the dreaded emergency ascent skill that bounces instructors up and down with each student. I was fatigued and dehydrated before the dive and had been doing two to three dives a day for over a week. Have I been hit with decompression sickness, or did I sprain my ankle jumping from the boat? It's probably the latter, but I can't rule out the worst possibility.

Few divers have seen someone with the bends, but bends paranoia runs rampant among them. We have all heard horror stories as well as having learned about it in our certification course. Fear lurks somewhere in every divers mind after a reasonably deep dive. For every tingle, ache, or itch, there is always an introspective period of hesitant concern until the ailment disappears.

227

Bends symptoms are caused by bubble formation in the blood and usually set on gradually after the end of a dive. Common ailments are itching, tingling, or joint pain. The term is descriptive – stricken divers often bend their elbows to ease the pain. In extreme cases, divers have keeled over into unconsciousness. Some have died. Ideally, a patient should go to a recompression chamber as soon as possible. The pressure inside reduces bubble volume and allows pure oxygen treatments to work more effectively. Breathing oxygen is the miracle cure, allowing bubbles to filter out through respiration. I've felt tingly or dizzy several times myself, but never enough to send me running for an oxygen bottle.

People get the bends from ascending too quickly, staying down too long, going to high altitude after diving, or other contributing factors (fatigue, dehydration, cold, obesity, exercise, alcohol consumption, and unique medical conditions). Half of the victims I've met got bent by deep diving with hangovers. Worn out from late night drinking, their bodies were dried out and had strange chemicals floating around from alcohol breaking down. They were diving side by side with buddies without hangovers who didn't get hit.

A customer told me he went to the chamber in Guam once *for* a hangover. After the first dive, he felt horrible. The chamber was nearby, so they chucked him in. After they took him down, he still felt like hell. Aspirin and hair of the dog were the only things that helped.

An adventurous American diver in Saint Lucia gave us a sobering lesson about following the rules. He turned up at our shop and asked for dives deeper than 130 feet. Being so close to the land of litigation (the US), he was abruptly denied. He left in a huff and took his tank elsewhere to be filled. After hiring local fishermen to take him out to the reef in a canoe, he set out alone for the dive of a lifetime.

At 307 feet, he was stoned on narcosis. After ascending to 250 feet, he ran out of air. When he took his last breath, he realized he was screwed, dropped his weights, and somehow made it back. Unfortunately, he got bent like a pretzel. He arrived at the chamber in Barbados in agony, his body turning black and blue from bubbles rupturing his blood vessels. Two weeks later, after daily treatments, he still couldn't walk without assistance.

His scuba gear was returned to our shop for examination because we had handled the evacuation logistics and needed to file a report. After removing his regulator, we turned the tank valve on. There was a minuscule hiss. Faced with the very real terror of drowning, Mr. Bubble had sucked as hard as he could. There wasn't enough air left for a mouse to breathe.

Anyway, my ankle isn't feeling better, but at least it hasn't gotten worse. If I do develop more symptoms, I'm going to be in big trouble. I'm in such an isolated area that getting to the nearest chamber will be an odyssey from hell, involving horse carts, boats, busses, bemos, and possibly trains or helicopters. I think this is as bad as it will get, so I'll lie here for a day or two instead and wait for my ankle to heal on its own.

COTILLION
Gili Air, Indonesia

"Remember when sex was safe and diving was dangerous?"
bumper sticker

Sunday. The Immigration Gestapo showed up, seized my passport, and ordered me to appear downtown the following morning. How much did they want this time? Were they going to deport me? Adi, Rudy, and the boys decided on a definite probably, so just in case, we planned a farewell beach party for my last night.

Around the campfire, Rudy and I strummed our best chords under the influence of rice-wine coolers. Ina, an attractive German tourist, was making googly eyes at me across the fire's flames. Her long blonde hair accented the fresh tan of her face and bare shoulders. She cheered my acoustic rendition of the Offspring's "Come Out and Play," but as the grog took its toll, our musical talents vaporized. The boys packed it in as the coals withered in the sand. Ina took a few steps down the beach and glanced back to me. I went after her.

"Don't ask me to go for a walk."

"I wasn't going to. Let's go for a dive."

We hooked up tanks and each grabbed a mask, leaving flashlights behind because of the full moon overhead. I peeled off my shirt. She dropped her sarong. The water was warm and inviting. Together we swam to the base of the reef.

At sixty feet, the moonlight on the white sand of the bottom provided all the light we needed. Green sparkles of bioluminescence flowed around us. Inspired, I took her hand in mine and led a tango across the sand. Dip? No problem. As I swung her low, miniature emerald embers swirled from her hair, highlighting our gliding limbs with a tiny glow.

Swish. Whirl. Spin. No longer slaves to gravity, our dance went into three dimensions. Sideways sambas. Upside-down waltzes. Oblique-angled lambadas. After an hour, we surfaced. Shivering in the night breeze, we retreated to the shelter of my bungalow.

BABES IN THAILAND
Phuket

"I just feel like I'm on this roller coaster of bar girls, and strange squiggly signs, and weird vehicles, and more bar girls, and Mai Tais. What the fuck am I doing here?" Billy

Welcome to a developing country. They've installed western toilets over the hole in the floor in some places, but they still squat with their feet on the seat when they use them.

Phuket Island is pronounced poo-ket, not that other word you were just thinking. I scored work at a dive shop on Patong Beach my first day in town.

Ten years ago, Patong was beach bars and bungalows connected by dirt roads. Huge hotels have appeared since to create the new "Riviera" of Southeast Asia. Ramshackle architecture flew up without a hint of civic planning – as if it were designed during a fourth-grade class project. Buildings were apparently constructed by out-of-work dormitory builders on a budget. Chaotic disarrays of Christmas lights illuminate small businesses. What's the national hobby? Amateur electronics?

A mysterious green/brown slime streaks down the concrete walls of every building. A combination of algae, mold, smoke, smog, and dirt is my guess. If the city ever shuts off the streetlights, it will probably creep out into the roadway as well.

Shrines are everywhere: in stairwells, in front of businesses, inside homes, and impromptu places such as the beach. They are placed on the floor, bolted to the wall, or mounted on pedestals. An ornate miniature house is usually part of the display. Offerings for Buddha are left in front of each. Usually incense is burning in a jar full of sand, and strings of fresh flowers are placed along the sides of the midget temple.

233

The shrine in my apartment lobby this morning featured two pieces of toast, a butter knife, and a little tray full of butter and jam. A few ants were investigating the offerings in hopes that Buddha wouldn't get there first. There was also an open Coke with a straw in it. I don't know if Buddha prefers straws, or if that is just typical Thai politeness.

Patong is predominately a winter getaway for Europeans who thrive on darkening their doughy hides during the Mediterranean off-season. For some reason, having sagging wrinkled bodies doesn't dampen the modesty of the over-fifty crowd on the beach. Skimpy bikini tops are flaunted *haute couture* over immense breasts and men's butt cracks peak out from alarmingly undersized Lycra briefs. There are also plenty of single men and their Thai dates. Despite the availability of parasailing, windsurfing, and jet skiing, the preferred distraction is relaxing in rented beach chairs and drinking.

There is an abundance of Indian tailors, all advertising "authentic" replications of Daniel Hechter, Giorgio Armani, or Ralph Lauren. Glass storefronts exhibit a lineup of grotesquely pale mannequins sporting suits that would have horrified Captain Kangaroo. As someone approaches, the merchants go into their routine. "Bongiorno, Bonjour, Guten Morgen, Good Morning, how are you sir? Please come look inside. Special price today." I have no idea how they stay in business. The only big sale I ever witnessed was a pair of hot pink dinner jackets with matching pants for a gay couple.

Every day is Sunday and every night is Saturday night in this makeshift sleaze pit. The main drag is Soi Bangla, home to girlie bars, drunken tourists, and a rag tag mish-mash of foreign residents. During the day, the vacant strip is impassable because it reeks with every possible organic excretion, but for some reason, the smell vanishes at night when the sidewalks and bars are packed to capacity.

A girlie bar is a small three or four-sided outdoor bar with a roof. Any of the dozen or so barmaids will go home with you if asked. They range in age from too young to too old, but their reasons for being there are not so diverse. They come with hopes and dreams for a better future, and for money, of course. A hard working hustler can easily make more than a doctor or college professor in Thailand.

When young girls roll in from the countryside dressed in T-shirts and flip-flops, their mentors take them in and turn them on to make-up, high heels, low-cut dresses, and the tricks of the hustle. Many tell a sob story: dead father, decrepit mother, and seven younger siblings to support or send to school. "Oh, by the way, can you pay my rent for me this month?" It's a hard line to believe sometimes. The girls range from sad and misplaced to happy and in their element. Most of them are out to have fun, and do. Said one, "I have smiles and happiness and freedom all the time." Many meet husbands and pack it in for the good life in Europe, America, or Australia. The downside is that many also end up stuck in town, turned harder than granite after too many cycles of heartbreak from an endless parade of uncaring men. Chain smoking, alcoholism, VD, and pregnancy are other vocational hazards.

There is a booming business of transsexual cabarets. The Thai transvestites ("kat-hoy" in Thai), don't just grow their hair long, wear make-up, and cross dress. Sex change specialists convert their genitalia to replicate a woman's. Silicone chest and butt implants create licentious bulges and curves. Most Thai women are skinny enough to stand sideways and hide behind light poles, so the transsexuals stand out as the most voluptuous women in the country. Still, closer inspection reveals that something is not quite right. Their shoulders may be too broad or square, or their feet may be too big. The Adam's apple may be prominent, and some needed a shave. The biggest giveaways are deep voices and walking postures. Only women can stroll like women. Kathoy push it too hard. Their limp-wristed hip-swinging strut can be spotted from three-hundred yards out.

During my first trip to Thailand, I was dumbstruck by a bikini-clad beauty standing in front of a club – tall, lean, and built like a Ferrari. As I walked past, she saw me staring and said hello. When her gravely baritone hit my ears, my hair stood on end, and I jumped out of my flip-flops. It took a few weeks of ogling my own gender before I learned the telltale signs. The worst part was that my confidence was blown. Every time I saw a sexy woman, I'd have doubts about whether I should be attracted or not until she was thoroughly checked out and verified.

When the US Navy sails in, the town goes crazy. Thousands of marines and sailors hit the bars looking to "grab a Thai-girl by the tail." The night strip opens six hours early, and truckloads of extra beer are brought in. One of the girlie bars on Bangla is not a girlie bar at all. It is a kathoy bar, and a great place to watch from across the street when the fleet is in. One of their gimmicks is topless dancing. Bouncing brown silicone breasts draw crowds out to the sidewalk. Nineteen-year-old drunken sailors are not very good at recognizing transsexuals. They weave happily into the bar with their eyes bugging out, sometimes hugging, nuzzling, or even kissing. Almost always, one of the sailors will realize what's going on and suddenly get very sober. "Guys! Hey, guys! We gotta go! We're going, now! No, no, don't wait a minute. Come on. Now!" as he tugs on sleeves and pulls his buddies back to safety.

Students often come to class exhausted and mentally absent from a big night out, but at least they have an excuse. The expatriates that live here year round are always this way. Efficiency, punctuality, reliability, good grooming, and consideration all go down the drain after they spend a few years in this sultry environment. I don't know if it's because of the lethargic, indigenous culture, or if it's just their way of dealing with the bizarre environment. Perhaps it's because Patong attracts a lot of screwballs, and they were already wacky when they arrived. They usually fit more than one of the following descriptions:

(in descending order)

Large Business Owners: These guys almost always have Thai wives and a few half-Thai kids running around. Their businesses support their families, and local connections make things easier for growth.

Small Business Owners: Few make huge profits here. Those who don't, make barely enough to continue living in Thailand. Some supplement their income with ventures back home.

Dawdling Expatriates: People who simply like it better here, or aren't welcome at home. Most get by on savings. Some have trust funds, illicit earnings, or inheritances. Many try to assimilate themselves into the culture by speaking Thai and acting Thai, but it never really works.

Butterflies: Most of these guys like having a variety of women, but are too old or unattractive to do this at home without spending a fortune. Although called butterflies by the girls in reference to bouncing from flower to flower, most are, in fact, helicopters. Some playboys love to be number one at their regular hangouts. They squander money on every woman in each place, winning popularity contests, and creating devout fan clubs of sexy companions.

Barflies: What better place to be a lounge lizard? An international subculture of boozers inhabits the bars twenty-four hours a day, sucking down the cheap liquor as fast as it's poured. Nobody enforces drinking laws (I don't even know if they exist) so anyone can roam the streets holding an open bottle.

Others, including most of the dive instructors, are just passing through.

⇜ ⇜ ⇜

My friend Dave just rolled in for a visit from the States, incredibly stressed out from weary working conditions, and complaining of his recent breakup with his girlfriend. After hearing him out, I proclaim, "You've come to the right place to be cured. Let the doctor take over." My first prescription is a bottle of Mekong* whiskey, a liter of Coke, and a tub of ice on

237

the neighboring Club Med beach. Attitude adjustment hour is a success, highlighted by French women strolling past in thong bikini bottoms.

*Mekong whisky is semi-hallucinogenic rice liquor — seventy proof, and evil, evil, evil. Mixed fifty-fifty with Coke, it can hardly be tasted because of its sweetness. The effects creep up slowly as innocent victims guzzle. The first time I drank a hip flask, I found myself pinned to the bed, staring at my hotel room's drapes blowing in the wind. The Mekong caused them to spiral like a barber pole. My eyes were transfixed on the rotating pattern as it spun slowly up the curtain. After reaching the top, it dropped to the base, as if commanded, for another ride up the tapestry. I was a slave to a piece of cotton cloth. After a half hour, I finally peeled my gaze away, only to go out and get some more Mekong.

The doctor decrees that the next therapy session is to be held in a sunset bar where the beer taps never close. There is only one place to hammer cheap draft beers with the big boys. By big, I mean the rotund merrymakers of the Sonnenbrand army. The beachhead invasion point is the Biergarten, a happy-hour bratwurst grill/open-air saloon stuffed with fat German couples. The husbands are shirtless, but the wives wear tiny wraps. Barely concealed, their bulbous Free Willy tits jiggle with every laugh. Thai girls in T-shirts flash charming smiles as they fill mugs. German folk music clamors. (What the hell was that? An accordion solo?) The guy to my right is obviously new in town because he is sober at this hour and politely asks to read the German newspaper lying in front of me. The last rays of the sun angle across the bar as we hold our own. Dave is on the stool to my left. Beyond him, a homogenous blend of Deutschland's best business walruses line the bar in their Speedos while they boisterously quaff. Tanning oil glints from their broad shoulders as they hoist another Krugful to their pudgy faces. At the end of the bar is a couple old enough to have several sets of grandkids. The man is drunkenly kissing his immense wife in a drawn out slurp. She chuckles out cigarette smoke as their lips part and flicks some sort of harmless flying insect off his shoulder. Gemütlichkeit. Everybody is happy but nobody is dancing on the picnic tables yet. Perhaps the beer mugs aren't big enough.

It's dark. We're hammered. On the busy street outside, it's time for the next prescription.

"What now, doctor?"

"To the girlie bars, young David!"

I hop on the scooter.

Dave strolls confidently into the street saying, "I'll stop traffic so you can pull out."

"Don't! Come back and get on the bike."

Ignoring his doctor's order, the innocent hero does his best New York traffic cop imitation. Confused tuk-tuk drivers and motorcyclists are baffled as they use him for a slalom gate. Dave stands amidst the bedlam like a confused matador while I laugh myself silly.

I haul my ward up to the girlie strip and introduce him to some of my favorites. The girls are playing the devious hammer game. They're betting a beer they can win. There's a trick, of course; the nail must be driven into a rock hard tree stump with the wedge-shaped peen of a blacksmithing hammer.

Dave says, "I'll take 'em on. I'm a construction worker."

"Careful, Dave. These girls do this every night."

He takes ten hits to drive his sixteen-penny nail. The girl does it in eight and, not surprisingly, collects cash instead of liquid.

On to the go-gos. (We give the transsexual cabarets a miss.) I know the perfect spot — the country and western place. Women clad in the last dying threads of cut-off-above-the-hip-pockets Levi's are pivoting on the heels of their knee-high leather boots. Staring seductively from under the brims of their cowboy hats, they check us out for any indication of affluence. Dave and I hoist ourselves onto stools under the runway. Achy Breaky Heart pounds out of the speakers. A braless honey sporting a ripped-up fishnet blouse gives us a wink.

My patient throws a glance in my general direction and shouts, "This place is so sleazy."

"Don't think of it as sleaze. Think of it as good for morale."

He gives me a that-was-funny grimace. "But I hate country music."

"You'll get used to it."

My patient is amazed by their hip gyrations but feels guilty about staring. I don't. I know talent when I see it. How exactly did my downfall occur . . . and when?

Dave mutters in astonishment, "She's using the pole."

I nod silently without shifting my gaze.

After awhile, I yell, "Hey Dave. I think I'll write a story about transsexual stalkers who abduct dive instructors, hide them in dreary concrete apartment blocks in Patong, and subject them to the continual barking of their mutant poodles until they guzzle Carlsberg, grow their hair long, and stop cutting their toenails. What d'ya think?"

"Excellent!"

I'm wondering how I can incorporate space aliens into the plot somewhere when Dave looks over and yells, "Why do I love this?"

They boot us out at closing time, so we drift off-balance across the street to the four-in-the-morning strip only to be assaulted by seven-year-olds peddling roses, Chiclets, and cigarettes. After telling them firmly in English to go home and go to bed because tomorrow is a school day, we head back to the scooter.

Into the parking area rides the sexiest doll of the night. Dave's mouth drops open. She notices and flashes a million-dollar smile. She accepts a drink invitation and he goes off with her in a euphoric cloud of white picket fences and 2.3 kids. The trouble is, she's floating on a cloud of "I'm gonna make fifty bucks tonight." He is a perfect gentleman in the bar and never gets down to business. After awhile, she moves on to greener pastures. He thinks he struck out, so I explain that she's a cash-first kind of girl.

"She's a what? No way. She's way too nice for that. No way. I don't believe you. She's so sweet! Get outta here. How can you say such a thing?"

Read it and weep, brother, and don't forget to listen to your doctor.

᷃ ᷃ ᷃

It's noon again, somehow. Dave and I are headed down the beach for Tabernack's, a bar run by a free-swilling misplaced French Canadian who came with visions of grandeur, but ended up drinking his profits. (His nickname is Tabernacle, a rude word in Quebecois.) He knows how to treat us right by pouring icy draught beer into frozen mugs. We're hoping to catch his big North-American-style breakfast omelet, as well. There's a Buddhist shrine under a tree to our right that looks more like a birdhouse on a plywood platform. Somebody lopped the top off a coconut with a machete and stuck a straw in the hole. Buddha has had his fill of coconut milk today, apparently, because it's still full. Dave is also satiated — and recovering nicely.

THE TWILIGHT ZONE
Krabi, Thailand

"Expect the unexpected." Proverb

Panicking divers can easily kill themselves by breath holding. As the pressure decreases during an ascent, the air volume increases, causing over-pressurization and lung rupture — almost always fatal. Instructors are therefore trained to hold frantic divers down until they start breathing through a regulator again.

Anna and her husband, Richard, were the only students in my course. One of the exercises they had to do taught the effects of lung volume on buoyancy. It is executed by lying face down on the bottom, holding the body rigid, and slowly inhaling to float up like an opening door, using the fins as hinges, then exhaling to sink. During skill demonstrations on the first dive, Anna laid down in the sand, floated up, then exhaled. Instead of sinking like she was supposed to, she put her hands down and stopped. I motioned for her to try again. After two more attempts, she was still putting her hands down. With a shrug, I asked what was wrong. She pointed at the sand. I assumed that the dead coral chunks were too sharp for her liking, so I laid my arms out to give her a soft place to land. She lay down on them, floated up again, then sat on her knees. When I looked at her face, I saw she was crying and hyperventilating. I gave her an "are you okay?" signal, and she glared at me hatefully. Then, like a child throwing a tantrum, she turned and started swimming out to sea.

I grabbed her tank valve, motioned for Richard to follow, and guided her to the surface. After she calmed down, I asked, "What's wrong?"

"I can't help thinking that there is something in the sand that is going to come out and eat me."

I paused, racking my brain for an answer. "Okay, forget that skill. Let's move on"

I was reluctant to proceed because of her freak out, but she insisted that she was okay. I gave a pep talk on staying calm and we resumed the dive.

Because of the vertical reef, the only practice area was forty feet deep. When she was ready, I signaled for her to simulate an out-of-air emergency. She calmly removed the regulator from her mouth and signaled, "I'm out of air" to Richard. As he passed her his spare regulator, it free-flowed, causing bubbles to hit her face.

She panicked.

Without a regulator, she held her breath and clawed wildly for the surface. I held her down, grabbed her regulator with my free hand, rammed it into her mouth, and hit the purge button. After four seemingly endless seconds, she stopped thrashing around and started breathing. I relaxed my grip as my own terror subsided. I was shaky and felt nauseous. We called it quits, headed back to the boat, and had a long talk about the incident.

"Anna, it's okay. You don't have to do this. Diving is not for everyone."

THE SENSITIVE AUSSIE
Similan Islands, Thailand

"... the ranting American cried, 'You're on the wrong track wanting only English settlers! Why, in my veins there runs the blood of Armenians, Russians, Turks, Irish, Germans and Czechoslovakians.' From the rear of the (Australian) audience came a whisper... 'By Jove! His mother was a sporting sort...'" Michener

A newcomer walking into a pub in Australia won't wait long before receiving what is commonly known as a ration of shit. This is known as "stirring" (pronounced "steren,") the Australian national sport. Basically, it's just wising off to someone you know or just met in a good-natured manner. In most parts of the world, this is called picking a fight. To the Aussies, it's their way of establishing rapport and making friends. Stirring contests can get vicious, but the Aussies are thick skinned. Instead of getting mad, they get even by exchanging progressively wittier quips. Once you figure out their language and play along, you'll have a great time, but don't plan on winning. When I first went to Oz, I tried wising off in return, but quickly learned that I couldn't compete with pros. When I meet Aussies overseas now, the first thing I do is get a jab in with my best wise crack, then quit while I'm ahead.

Years later, I went to the Similan Islands to work on a live-aboard dive boat. There were two other divemasters on the boat: Steve, an American who ran the trip, and Mick from Australia. A noticeable feature on Mick's head was a scar that showed through his crewcut.

We checked out equipment to new customers one morning while I wrote down colors and sizes on a clipboard, and Mick handed out the gear. Within minutes, one of the customers had misplaced his fins. Steve came over and asked what color they were.

Mick said, "Black."

I looked at the clipboard and said that they were fluorescent yellow. I also remembered this because I had to raise my yellow tinted sunglasses to check.

Mick insisted on black.

I said, "Yellow."

Steve said, "Well, which is it? I've got to know."

Mick said black again.

Steve looked back at me and I couldn't resist.

I pointed at Mick's scar and said, "You know how we got circumcised at home when we were born? Well, In Australia, they do something different. Instead of removing foreskins, they remove half of the brain."

That got him. He was not only speechless, he looked hurt. I apologized, but I couldn't believe it.

I had found a sensitive Australian.

THE PHUKET GRAND PRIX
Thailand

"I'm not sure if these guys are the world's worst drivers or the best." Dave

"You never really learn to swear until you learn to drive." Anonymous

Welcome to the daily road race of Thailand, the Phuket Grand Prix, where the only rule is:

Whoever passes the most cars, wins.

Typical road behavior is best summarized by the art of high-speed tailgating — standard foreplay before passing any vehicle. After getting within inches of the car in front, drivers whip around either side and play chicken with any oncoming traffic. Why these people, who spend most of their day studying their fingernails or sleeping, become hell bent behind a steering wheel is beyond me. It must be the only form of excitement they get. All drivers share one characteristic — no apparent fear of death.

Thais don't learn to drive at driving schools. They learn from their parents, who as far as I can tell, take them to carnival bumper car rides for their first lesson. This is a good thing because their parents were good enough at survival driving to live long enough to reproduce.

The Thais tend to drive wherever they can, sidewalks included. Why they bothered to paint center lines in the road is almost as funny as the painted arrows pointing the wrong way. Long ago, someone devised a master plan for traffic routing in the town and had the official road directions changed to a system of one way streets. This was subsequently ignored, but the arrows remained.

The streets are full of odd vehicles: The world's smallest taxis, called tuk-tuks, look like a cross between a rickshaw and a trash dumpster. They get their name from their three-cylinder engines sputtering out *tuk tuk tuk* as they zip through any available gap in the traffic. Cars range from Mercedes Benzes to refrigerator sized Daihatsus. Mobile food-vendor scooters putt down the road with their sidecar "shops," functioning as moving slalom gates for teenage males on motorcycles hopped up to match the pace of their hormones.

90cc Honda scooters comprise eighty percent of the traffic. At red lights, their drivers zip past stopped cars to the front of the queue and wait with anxious eyes on the signal in the cross direction. When the yellow light turns, they jump their green to form a huge jousting match as they dodge everybody running the light in the cross-direction. Then there's a fight for dominance as people make turns across traffic before it's clear.

Fitting as many people as possible onto a motorcycle is a popular hobby. The record to beat for total motorcycle passengers at once is six, counting babies, but not dogs. They apparently bring their entire family with them so if there is a fatal accident, nobody is left to bear the misery.

Driving a motorcycle here is like being in the middle of a football game during kickoff. Confused bodies fly in all directions. Some swarm past from behind, several at a time, while others come head-on, or stop in the middle of the lane. To complicate matters, there are cars, busses, and very big trucks that are all trying to go faster than the motorcycles. Staying alert is mandatory because lethal menaces abound:

- dogs trot into the road;
- drivers almost always pull out without looking;
- phone poles, signposts and fire hydrants are sometimes located in the middle of lanes;
- manhole covers and drainage grates vanish;
- sections of road drop into culverts, leaving chasms big enough to swallow an entire Honda.

The two biggest imponderables are mothers driving scooters with their right hand on the throttle while carrying a baby in their left arm and people driving against traffic in the wrong lane. Stupidity is the key here, I think. The lack of foresight on behalf of the mothers I can almost understand, but when I asked why cyclists go head on with oncoming traffic, I received this answer. "They are only going a short distance, so they don't waste time by crossing over into their lane." As far as I can tell, "a short distance" on Thai roads is anything less than a mile.

The brake pedal seems to be located at the center of the steering wheel and is used several times a minute. A beeping horn usually means "you will die now if you ignore me." Honk before passing, honk before going around curves, honk before passing on curves, honk to warn people not to pull out, honk to say hi, but don't honk at dogs in the road – that would be silly.

Annoyances include stinky black diesel exhaust and speed bumps spaced forty feet apart in alleys. The latter are built high enough to sand steel filings from every passing undercarriage. Some are located at the end of cul-de-sacs, where, as everyone knows, people love to speed.

The traffic police don't do much except enforce the helmet law within a hundred feet of their checkpoint. All motorcycle drivers, but not passengers, must have head protection (fastened straps optional). After leaving the enforcement area, drivers return their hard hats to their handlebar baskets. Anybody caught and fined does not need to wear a helmet for the rest of the day. A general amnesty is also granted on Buddhist holidays.

Are there accidents? Of course! The hospital is filled with battered road victims. For some reason, the police spray-paint the outlines of crashed vehicles onto the road. These "murder scene" diagrams appear in the street with unnerving regularity.

For some added amusement, throw a dive instructor from Los Angeles into the melee behind the wheel of a songthaew lek (pickup truck with a canopy and seats in back). Can he drive his students from the dive shop to the beach without getting everyone killed in a crash with an ice cream cart? With his native defensive driving skills, he might be able to make it.

You can take the boy out of L.A., but you can't take the L.A. out of the boy. Los Angeles drivers honk when they're pissed off at the way someone is driving. They also yell nasty things and use rude finger gestures. The polite Thais would never dream of doing anything so crass. This means I can freely vent anger without encountering opposition. It doesn't do anything for international relations, but it keeps me sane.

Some sample encounters:

Me

Hey, ass wipe, you're going the wrong way in my lane. Oh, am I in your way? Where'd ya learn to drive, anyway? The back of a Captain Crunch cereal box?

Other driver

(friendly smile)

Me

Hey numb nuts, you happen to be passing me on a curve. Has it occurred to you that you're about to kill us all, you dick brain?

Other driver

(friendly smile)

One morning on the way to the beach with my class, I was undergoing the normal road stress in the songthaew lek and muttering some fairly good curses at appropriate times. My vulgarity climaxed as I approached a blind curve at the top of a hill and not one, but three motorists passed me at once. To top things off, two motorcyclists were passing on the shoulder to my left. With a crescendo of indecency, I generated a cloud of obscenity that is probably still hanging over that curve. What I had overlooked was that the window was down. My students in back could hear everything I was yelling. They never mentioned it afterward. I never asked.

THE NUTTY AUSSIE
Phuket, Thailand

"You can always tell a maniac by the way he laughs." Hoyt

The dive shop manager called one night and asked if I could fill in for an instructor who had inexplicably disappeared in mid-course. In the morning, I met his student, Greg.

"Hi, I'm Mike."

"Good day, Mick. You always get your hair done by Shirley Temple's beautician?"

"Oh, an Aussie, that explains it. Where you from?"

"Brisbane."

"Isn't that near that outback place where all the sheep are scared."

"Hey, I never met one that complained."

"Right. Are you ready to go?"

"I'm nervous."

"So am I."

"No, seriously. I'm really nervous." He was suddenly earnest.

"Oh, sorry. I thought you were still kidding. There's nothing to worry about. We'll take it nice and easy. Just let me know what you feel comfortable with."

"How can I trust you?"

That stopped me for a second, so I began relating my years of experience. His face twitched with apprehension, and warning bells sounded in my mind. "Is something bothering you?"

"I almost drowned as a child, and I'm really terrified of water."

"Then why are you taking a dive course?"

"My girlfriend thinks I'm afraid to try it. She's a diver and gave me a dive course for Christmas last year but I blew it off. I

251

thought I'd do it now to make it up to her. I also want to get over my hang-up about going into deep water."

I could tell he wasn't cut out for diving, but if he wanted to conquer fears, fine. After all, I could hardly argue myself out of two days work.

Everyone is a little crazy. It's the maniacs you have to watch out for. Greg had a wild drawn-out laugh. Like many Australians, he took an opportunity to wise off when he could, but his humor was a little too far removed from reality to be funny.

On the way to the beach, he kept shouting out the truck window at anything resembling a German couple. "Hey Hansel! Hey Gretel!"

"Hey, what's with you and Germans?" I asked.

"Yermans?"

"Germans."

"Mermen?"

This guy was hardly Bill Murray. I suspected why his previous instructor had disappeared.

We learned in our divemaster course that nervousness before a dive can cause strange effects on otherwise normal people. Over the years I had seen people turn snotty, giggle stupidly, stall for time, or shake with fear. Talkative people go silent, quiet people turn loquacious, and others flat out refuse to put their equipment on. Normally when I see this, I comfort them. If they don't want to go, it's okay. If they do go, I try to get them calmed down before they get in the water. I wondered what the hell was going on with Greg.

Our first dive went straight out from the beach along the edge of a reef. When we dropped down to the sand on scuba, he suddenly started acting like John Belushi in Animal House checking to see if the coast was clear in front of the dean's office. As we moved down the reef, he'd spin suddenly to see what might be coming up behind him. After a few seconds of searching the blue for invaders, he'd whirl back to join me again. He was fifteen feet deep on a calm sunny day acting like he was going through a hall of horrors. After ten minutes, he

252

started pointing frantically back in the direction of the beach. I thought it was silly to end the dive, but went back anyway.

Back on dry land, I asked, "Why did you want to come out so early?"

"I felt like I was lost."

For somebody who was lost, he sure knew where that beach was.

On the way home, Greg invited me to his room for a cocktail. I figured this might be the only tip I was going to get, so I took him up on it.

In the hotel elevator, Greg lit up when an older German couple came in on the second floor. "Hello, Bertha! Hello, Adolf!"

The man looked surprised, "Excuse me, sir?"

Greg stifled a snigger by snorting through his nose. The man went red with anger. I hid my face in the corner.

When we stepped out, Greg smiled and waved back to the couple. "All feet are the same!"

The elevator doors closed.

"What did you say?"

"That's Yerman for 'Goodbye.'"

In his room, Greg offered premium whiskey and a game of chess. I settled for beer and let him play white. Greg powered back two stiff ones on the rocks in ten minutes. When I said checkmate, he launched himself over the bed to the center of the room and sprang up facing me in a karate stance. I guessed he was doing the Bruce Lee thing for my benefit and jumped up also. He threw a head high roundhouse kick at me. I ducked it and threw up my arm. His ankle smacked the dive watch off my wrist.

His eyes were gleaming and he was smiling maniacally.

"Are you nuts?" I asked in disbelief.

He stayed in his fighting stance.

I picked up my watch and left.

He didn't mention it the next morning, so I left it alone. Everything was under control until he got on the boat and greeted the German divemaster. "Good Morning, Adolf!"

The DM looked back. "I'm sorry, my name is Udo."

Greg snickered, and I disappeared astern, hoping not to be associated with him.

During the first dive, he was fidgeting like the bait boy in a Jaws movie, so I monitored him closely, fearing that he was going to freak out. I was relieved when the dive ended without incident.

Back on the boat, I ditched Greg and headed straight for the lunch table. (Divemaster rule #6b: they're not going to give you any more money, so the more you eat, the more you get paid.)

When we were ready for his final certification dive, Greg wouldn't jump in. The Thai crew was getting irritated because they needed to move the boat. I wanted him to go so I could get rid of him at the end of the day. He said he wanted to finish, so we all waited as he stood up, sighed, sat down, caught some fresh air, spit in his mask, stood up, sat down, et cetera. The boat boy was the first to blow his stack.

Thais are usually pretty mellow dudes, but this one ran up shouting, "Go now! Go!"

That pissed Greg off.

The sixteen-year-old Thai got right in his face. "Why you look me like that?"

Greg cocked his fist and was about to knock the scrawny kid the length of the deck when I jumped in between.

I should have pushed Greg overboard and solved everyone's problem.

Back at the dock, I offered to let him continue the course.

"No, that's all right. I've had enough. Thanks."

The last time I saw him, he was walking down the seawall, grinning back at the divemaster. "Hey Adolf! All feet are the same!"

EPILOGUE
Gili Air, Indonesia

"When no business, Mike stress. When too much business, Mike go crazy." Suno

Adi whipped my butt in chess again this evening because I was drinking jungle juice. They make it from rice, but I don't know how they get it so strong without distilling it. Judging from the way it tastes, they probably add Windex. I mix it with Coke to make it palatable.

I also had a relatively hard workday. Two Austrians insisted on bouncing over the reef like beach balls on a crowd of football fans. Their blood streaked shins didn't bother me nearly as much as the valley girl who wouldn't shut up about her regulator during pool training. "Is this thing working right? Oh my God! What's that funny noise? Is this thing okay?"

"Since you're having trouble getting used to it, why don't you practice by keeping it in your mouth."

Days like this really accelerate my burnout rate. Teaching the same course over and over doesn't help, either. Luckily, it's the end of the dive season here, and burnout *is* curable. I'm heading back to Thailand in a week and looking forward to a month of therapy before the season starts in Phuket. I'll spend a lot of time in my beach hammock, snuggling with my Thai girlfriend, Nam Fohn, while she feeds me mango, papaya, and pineapple, and waves down the beer vendors when they pass. That will get me re-energized in time.

But then again, it's another beautiful starry night on Gili Air, and I can hear the boys playing guitar on the beach. Rudy is singing Bob Marley's Redemption Song with a Sasak accent. Other than that, the only sounds are gecko chirps, the occasional rustle of leaves in the wind, and the low hiss of the kerosene lantern (the generators are off for the night). The claws of Scorpio are directly overhead, and the Southern Cross is framed by palm trees.

Long lazy nights like this are often a time for introspection. Where am I headed with this vagabond lifestyle, drifting from one spectacular dive locale to the next? I've spent three of the last thirty months in the States, and don't have any material gains except for a hodgepodge of passport stamps.

The last time I was visiting California, I wondered aloud to a friend, "What am I doing with my life?"

Without hesitation, he said, "Living it."

So, what next? I can't handle the isolation here. The wages in Thailand are lousy. The Caribbean pays well, but the diving doesn't compare. What about the Red Sea? Tons of Europeans go there to dive, and it has a reputation as one of the world's best places. A plane ticket out of Bangkok should be cheap. I'll look into it. Life with the Arabs. I wonder what that will be like . . .

GLOSSARY

Aussie Pronounced "Ozzie." An inhabitant of Australia, the Texas of the South Pacific.

Barrier Reef The outermost reef. It usually encircles an island, sheltering it from the waves breaking on the outer edge of the coral. The reef usually grows as close to the surface as possible — making it a great place to find shipwrecks. During very low tides (i.e. just after the moon is full or new), the coral may be above the surface.

BC Buoyancy compensator, a diver's inflatable vest. Contrary to the initial opinions of many students, it is not designed to be used as an elevator.

Bemo Indonesian version of a tuk-tuk. It isn't full if the door can still shut.

Bent Having decompression sickness (the bends). The term comes from victims who have painful bubbles in their joints, bending them to ease the anguish. When angry with divers, please don't tell them to "get bent." It is a sensitive issue.

Bottom Time The time from the start of the descent to the time of the final ascent to the surface. Ascent time is not calculated when using dive tables. Bottom time does not include decompression stops.

Bulletproof The state of intoxication that follows Invisible.

Computer Refers to a dive computer, a great toy that goes along on a dive to continually calculate the nitrogen uptake and release of the diver's tissues. Small enough to fit into a console or worn on a wrist.

Drift Line Hangs behind a boat that is anchored in a current. Divers can hold it while waiting for the dive to start to avoid being washed into the next country without a passport.

First Stage The regulator that attaches directly to the tank. A clever device that reduces the tank pressure to a much lower, hose pressure. Instructors love to control students by grabbing their first stages.

Haole Pronounced How-Lee. Hawaiian for (white) foreigner.

Hash House Harriers A world-wide expatriate running and beer-drinking cult. Also known as the Hash. Don't let any of them date your daughter.

High Pressure Hose Connects the tank pressure gauge to the first stage on the tank. Useful for dragging students around or subduing them.

I'm Beautiful The second state of intoxication after You're Beautiful.

Invisible The third state of intoxication after I'm Beautiful.

Lanai Hawaiian for porch.

Melanesia The Pacific cultural region that extends from Fiji to New Guinea. Also includes Vanuatu and the Solomon Islands.

Micronesia The Pacific cultural region that stretches from the Marshall Islands to the west of Hawaii to the Caroline Islands that end near the Philippines. Islands or countries mentioned in the text are Kwajalein, Ebeye, Kosrae, Ponape, Truk, Guam, Saipan, Yap, and Palau.

Mixed Gas Diving Introducing helium or other gases to the air mixture to reduce the effects of oxygen toxicity and nitrogen at depths greater than 190 feet, typically. Very technical stuff. Don't try it at home.

Nitrogen Narcosis An unexplained condition that effects divers at great depths. Often euphoric. See the chapter The Rapture of the Deep.

Octopus A spare second-stage regulator, often on a long hose, that a diver can give to an out of air diver. No, I don't know why it's called that.

Polynesia The Pacific cultural region that stretches from Hawaii to New Zealand. Other islands or countries mentioned in the text are Tahiti, the Cook Islands, Samoa, and Tonga.

Reverse Profile Visiting the deepest point of a dive just before surfacing. This effectively doubles the amount of residual nitrogen stored in a diver's body over the amount he would have if he had followed a proper deepest-point-first profile. See the chapter Bad Profiles.

Scuba Diving Diving with a tank on one's back. A self-contained-underwater-breathing-apparatus filled with air, NOT oxygen. Emile Gagnan and Jacques Cousteau invented the original "aqua-lung" in 1943.

Second Stage That thing that goes in your mouth. It works best under water when the tank valve is in the on position.

Skin Diving Another name for breath hold diving with a snorkel.

Tuk-Tuk A form of Thai public transport. Possibly the world's smallest taxi. An open air, three or four-wheeled miniature pickup-truck with a roof and a bench seat or two. Life insurance recommended before entry.

You're Beautiful The first state of intoxication (for those not drinking alone).

REFERENCES

Brower, Kenneth. *A Song for Satawal.* New York; Harper and Row, 1983

Chatwin, Bruce. *The Songlines.* New York; Penguin, 1987

Dyson, John. *Sink The Rainbow!* London; Victor Gollancz Ltd., 1986

Ross, Bill D. *A Special Piece of Hell.* New York; Saint Martin's Paperbacks, 1991

Stanley, David. *Micronesia Handbook.* Chico; Moon Publications, 1989

ABOUT THE AUTHOR

Michael Zinsley grew up in the Los Angeles area. He studied civil engineering and geology at the University of Colorado, Boulder, and then studied secondary education in graduate school at the California State University, Los Angeles. A seasoned traveler, he has been scuba diving in twenty-two different countries and has visited over eighty different countries and territories. He is also an accomplished mountaineer with notable ascents on five continents. Michael currently lives in Alameda, California. His writing has appeared in Skin Diver magazine and technical rock-climbing journals.

Printed in the United States
42435LVS00001B/91-117

The
Rapture of the Deep

AND OTHER

DIVE STORIES

You Probably Shouldn't Know